IELTS

ACADEMIC 18

WITH ANSWERS

AUTHENTIC PRACTICE TESTS

 WITH AUDIO

 CAMBRIDGE

WITH RESOURCE BANK

Shaftesbury Road, Cambridge CB2 8EA, United Kingdom

One Liberty Plaza, 20th Floor, New York, NY 10006, USA

477 Williamstown Road, Port Melbourne, VIC 3207, Australia

314–321, 3rd Floor, Plot 3, Splendor Forum, Jasola District Centre, New Delhi – 110025, India

103 Penang Road, #05–06/07, Visioncrest Commercial, Singapore 238467

Cambridge University Press & Assessment is a department of the University of Cambridge.

We share the University's mission to contribute to society through the pursuit of education, learning and research at the highest international levels of excellence.

www.cambridge.org
Information on this title: www.cambridge.org/9781009275187

© Cambridge University Press & Assessment 2023

First published 2023
20 19 18 17 16 15 14 13 12 11 10 9 8 7 6 5 4 3

Printed in Malaysia by Vivar Printing

A catalogue record for this publication is available from the British Library

ISBN 978-1-009-27518-7 Academic Student's Book with Answers with Audio with Resource Bank

Contents

Introduction

Prepare for the exam with practice tests from Cambridge

Inside you'll find four authentic examination papers from Cambridge University Press & Assessment. They are the perfect way to practise – EXACTLY like the real exam.

Why are they unique?

All our authentic practice tests go through the same design process as the IELTS test. We check every single part of our practice tests with real students under exam conditions, to make sure we give you the most authentic experience possible.

Students can take these tests on their own or with the help of a teacher to familiarise themselves with the exam format, understand the scoring system and practise exam technique.

Further information

IELTS is jointly managed by the British Council, IDP: IELTS Australia and Cambridge University Press & Assessment. Further information can be found on the IELTS official website at ielts.org.

WHAT IS THE TEST FORMAT?

IELTS consists of four components. All candidates take the same Listening and Speaking tests. There is a choice of Reading and Writing tests according to whether a candidate is taking the Academic or General Training module.

Academic	General Training
For candidates wishing to study at undergraduate or postgraduate levels, and for those seeking professional registration.	For candidates wishing to migrate to an English-speaking country (Australia, Canada, New Zealand, UK) and for those wishing to train or study below degree level.

The test components are taken in the following order:

Listening 4 parts, 40 items, approximately 30 minutes	
Academic Reading 3 sections, 40 items 60 minutes or	**General Training Reading** 3 sections, 40 items 60 minutes
Academic Writing 2 tasks 60 minutes or	**General Training Writing** 2 tasks 60 minutes
Speaking 11 to 14 minutes	
Total (Maximum) Test Time 2 hours 44 minutes	

ACADEMIC TEST FORMAT

Listening

This test consists of four parts, each with ten questions. The first two parts are concerned with social needs. The first part is a conversation between two speakers and the second part is a monologue. The final two parts are concerned with situations related to educational or training contexts. The third part is a conversation between up to four people and the fourth part is a monologue.

A variety of question types is used, including: multiple choice, matching, plan/map/ diagram labelling, form completion, note completion, table completion, flowchart completion, summary completion, sentence completion and short-answer questions.

Candidates hear the recording once only and answer the questions as they listen. Ten minutes are allowed at the end for candidates to transfer their answers to the answer sheet.

Reading

This test consists of three sections with 40 questions. There are three texts, which are taken from journals, books, magazines and newspapers. The texts are on topics of general interest. At least one text contains detailed logical argument.

A variety of question types is used, including: multiple choice, identifying information (True/False/Not Given), identifying the writer's views/claims (Yes/No/Not Given), matching information, matching headings, matching features, matching sentence endings, sentence completion, summary completion, note completion, table completion, flowchart completion, diagram-label completion and short-answer questions.

Writing

This test consists of two tasks. It is suggested that candidates spend about 20 minutes on Task 1, which requires them to write at least 150 words, and 40 minutes on Task 2, which requires them to write at least 250 words. Task 2 contributes twice as much as Task 1 to the Writing score.

Task 1 requires candidates to look at a diagram or some data (in a graph, table or chart) and to present the information in their own words. They are assessed on their ability to organise, present and possibly compare data, and are required to describe the stages of a process, describe an object or event, or explain how something works.

In Task 2, candidates are presented with a point of view, argument or problem. They are assessed on their ability to present a solution to the problem, present and justify an opinion, compare and contrast evidence and opinions, and evaluate and challenge ideas, evidence or arguments.

Candidates are also assessed on their ability to write in an appropriate style. More information on assessing the Writing test, including Writing assessment criteria (public version), is available at ielts.org.

Speaking

This test takes between 11 and 14 minutes and is conducted by a trained examiner. There are three parts:

Part 1

The candidate and the examiner introduce themselves. Candidates then answer general questions about themselves, their home/family, their job/studies, their interests and a wide range of similar familiar topic areas. This part lasts between four and five minutes.

Part 2

The candidate is given a task card with prompts and is asked to talk on a particular topic. The candidate has one minute to prepare and they can make some notes if they wish, before speaking for between one and two minutes. The examiner then asks one or two questions on the same topic.

Part 3

The examiner and the candidate engage in a discussion of more abstract issues which are thematically linked to the topic in Part 2. The discussion lasts between four and five minutes.

The Speaking test assesses whether candidates can communicate effectively in English. The assessment takes into account Fluency and Coherence, Lexical Resource, Grammatical Range and Accuracy, and Pronunciation. More information on assessing the Speaking test, including Speaking assessment criteria (public version), is available at ielts.org.

HOW IS IELTS SCORED?

IELTS results are reported on a nine-band scale. In addition to the score for overall language ability, IELTS provides a score in the form of a profile for each of the four skills (Listening, Reading, Writing and Speaking). These scores are also reported on a nine-band scale. All scores are recorded on the Test Report Form along with details of the candidate's nationality, first language and date of birth. Each Overall Band Score corresponds to a descriptive statement which gives a summary of the English-language ability of a candidate classified at that level. The nine bands and their descriptive statements are as follows:

9   **Expert user** – *Has fully operational command of the language: appropriate, accurate and fluent with complete understanding.*

8   **Very good user** – *Has fully operational command of the language with only occasional unsystematic inaccuracies and inappropriacies. Misunderstandings may occur in unfamiliar situations. Handles complex detailed argumentation well.*

7   **Good user** – *Has operational command of the language, though with occasional inaccuracies, inappropriacies and misunderstandings in some situations. Generally handles complex language well and understands detailed reasoning.*

6   **Competent user** – *Has generally effective command of the language despite some inaccuracies, inappropriacies and misunderstandings. Can use and understand fairly complex language, particularly in familiar situations.*

5   **Modest user** – *Has partial command of the language, coping with overall meaning in most situations, though is likely to make many mistakes. Should be able to handle basic communication in own field.*

4   **Limited user** – *Basic competence is limited to familiar situations. Has frequent problems in understanding and expression. Is not able to use complex language.*

3   **Extremely limited user** – *Conveys and understands only general meaning in very familiar situations. Frequent breakdowns in communication occur.*

2   **Intermittent user** – *Has great difficulty understanding spoken and written English.*

1   **Non-user** – *Essentially has no ability to use the language beyond possibly a few isolated words.*

0   **Did not attempt the test** – *Did not answer the questions.*

MARKING THE PRACTICE TESTS

Listening and Reading

The answer keys are on pages 119–126.
Each question in the Listening and Reading tests is worth one mark.

Questions which require letter / Roman numeral answers

For questions where the answers are letters or Roman numerals, you should write *only* the number of answers required. For example, if the answer is a single letter or numeral, you should write only one answer. If you have written more letters or numerals than are required, the answer must be marked wrong.

Questions which require answers in the form of words or numbers

- Answers may be written in upper or lower case.
- Words in brackets are *optional* – they are correct, but not necessary.
- Alternative answers are separated by a slash (/).
- If you are asked to write an answer using a certain number of words and/or (a) number(s), you will be penalised if you exceed this. For example, if a question specifies an answer using NO MORE THAN THREE WORDS and the correct answer is 'black leather coat', the answer 'coat of black leather' is *incorrect*.
- In questions where you are expected to complete a gap, you should only transfer the necessary missing word(s) onto the answer sheet. For example, to complete 'in the ...', where the correct answer is 'morning', the answer 'in the morning' would be *incorrect*.
- All answers require correct spelling (including words in brackets).
- Both US and UK spelling are acceptable and are included in the answer key.
- All standard alternatives for numbers, dates and currencies are acceptable.
- All standard abbreviations are acceptable.
- You will find additional notes about individual answers in the answer key.

Writing

The sample and model answers are on pages 127–137. It is not possible for you to give yourself a mark for the Writing tasks. We have provided sample answers (written by candidates), showing their score and the examiners' comments. We have also provided high-level model answers written by examiners. Additional sample and model answers can be downloaded from the Resource Bank. These sample and model answers will give you an insight into what is required for the Writing test.

HOW SHOULD YOU INTERPRET YOUR SCORES?

At the end of each Listening and Reading answer key you will find a chart which will help you assess whether, on the basis of your practice test results, you are ready to take the IELTS test.

In interpreting your score, there are a number of points you should bear in mind. Your performance in the real IELTS test will be reported in two ways: there will be a Band Score from 1 to 9 for each of the components and an Overall Band Score from 1 to 9, which is the average of your scores in the four components. However, institutions considering your application are advised to look at both the Overall Band Score and the Band Score for each component in order to determine whether you have the language skills needed for a particular course of study. For example, if your course involves a lot of reading and writing, but no lectures, listening skills might be less important and a score of 5 in Listening might be acceptable if the Overall Band Score was 7. However, for a course which has lots of lectures and spoken instructions, a score of 5 in Listening might be unacceptable even though the Overall Band Score was 7.

Once you have marked your tests, you should have some idea of whether your listening and reading skills are good enough for you to try the IELTS test. If you did well enough in one component, but not in others, you will have to decide for yourself whether you are ready to take the test.

The practice tests have been checked to ensure that they are the same level of difficulty as the real IELTS test. However, we cannot guarantee that your score in the practice tests will be reflected in the real IELTS test. The practice tests can only give you an idea of your possible future performance and it is ultimately up to you to make decisions based on your score.

Different institutions accept different IELTS scores for different types of courses. We have based our recommendations on the average scores which the majority of institutions accept. The institution to which you are applying may, of course, require a higher or lower score than most other institutions.

Test 1

PART 1   *Questions 1–10*

Complete the notes below.

*Write **ONE WORD AND/OR A NUMBER** for each answer.*

Listening test audio

Transport survey

Name: Sadie Jones

Year of birth: 1991

Postcode: **1** ....

Travelling by bus

Date of bus journey: **2** ....

Reason for trip: shopping and visit to the **3** ....

Travelled by bus because cost of   **4** .... too high

Got on bus at   **5** .... Street

Complaints about bus service: - bus today was **6** ....

                                - frequency of buses in the **7** ....

Travelling by car

Goes to the   **8** .... by car

Travelling by bicycle

Dislikes travelling by bike in the city centre because of the **9** ....

Doesn't own a bike because of a lack of **10** ....

PART 2   *Questions 11–20*

Questions 11–13

*Choose the correct letter, **A**, **B** or **C**.*

Listening test audio

Becoming a volunteer for ACE

11   Why does the speaker apologise about the seats?

    A   They are too small.
    B   There are not enough of them.
    C   Some of them are very close together.

12   What does the speaker say about the age of volunteers?

    A   The age of volunteers is less important than other factors.
    B   Young volunteers are less reliable than older ones.
    C   Most volunteers are about 60 years old.

13   What does the speaker say about training?

    A   It is continuous.
    B   It is conducted by a manager.
    C   It takes place online.

Questions 14 and 15

*Choose **TWO** letters, **A–E**.*

Which **TWO** issues does the speaker ask the audience to consider before they apply to be volunteers?

    A   their financial situation
    B   their level of commitment
    C   their work experience
    D   their ambition
    E   their availability

Questions 16–20

What does the speaker suggest would be helpful for each of the following areas of voluntary work?

Choose **FIVE** *answers from the box and write the correct letter,* **A–G**, *next to Questions 16–20.*

Helpful things volunteers might offer

A   experience on stage

B   original, new ideas

C   parenting skills

D   an understanding of food and diet

E   retail experience

F   a good memory

G   a good level of fitness

Area of voluntary work

16   Fundraising   ....

17   Litter collection   ....

18   'Playmates'   ....

19   Story club   ....

20   First aid   ....

PART 3   *Questions 21–30*

Questions 21–26

Choose the correct letter, A, B or C.

Listening test audio

Talk on jobs in fashion design

21   What problem did Chantal have at the start of the talk?

A   Her view of the speaker was blocked.
B   She was unable to find an empty seat.
C   The students next to her were talking.

22   What were Hugo and Chantal surprised to hear about the job market?

A   It has become more competitive than it used to be.
B   There is more variety in it than they had realised.
C   Some areas of it are more exciting than others.

23   Hugo and Chantal agree that the speaker's message was

A   unfair to them at times.
B   hard for them to follow.
C   critical of the industry.

24   What do Hugo and Chantal criticise about their school careers advice?

A   when they received the advice
B   how much advice was given
C   who gave the advice

25   When discussing their future, Hugo and Chantal disagree on

A   which is the best career in fashion.
B   when to choose a career in fashion.
C   why they would like a career in fashion.

26   How does Hugo feel about being an unpaid assistant?

A   He is realistic about the practice.
B   He feels the practice is dishonest.
C   He thinks others want to change the practice.

Questions 27 and 28

*Choose **TWO** letters, **A–E**.*

Which **TWO** mistakes did the speaker admit she made in her first job?

    A   being dishonest to her employer
    B   paying too much attention to how she looked
    C   expecting to become well known
    D   trying to earn a lot of money
    E   openly disliking her client

Questions 29 and 30

*Choose **TWO** letters, **A–E**.*

Which **TWO** pieces of retail information do Hugo and Chantal agree would be useful?

    A   the reasons people return fashion items
    B   how much time people have to shop for clothes
    C   fashion designs people want but can't find
    D   the best time of year for fashion buying
    E   the most popular fashion sizes

PART 4   *Questions 31–40*

Complete the notes below.

*Write **ONE WORD ONLY** for each answer.*

Listening test audio

Elephant translocation

Reasons for overpopulation at Majete National Park

- strict enforcement of anti-poaching laws

- successful breeding

Problems caused by elephant overpopulation

- greater competition, causing hunger for elephants

- damage to **31** .... in the park

The translocation process

- a suitable group of elephants from the same **32** .... was selected

- vets and park staff made use of **33** .... to help guide the elephants into an open plain

- elephants were immobilised with tranquilisers

  - this process had to be completed quickly to reduce **34** ....

  - elephants had to be turned on their **35** .... to avoid damage to their lungs

  - elephants' **36** .... had to be monitored constantly

  - tracking devices were fitted to the matriarchs

  - data including the size of their tusks and **37** .... was taken

- elephants were taken by truck to their new reserve

Advantages of translocation at Nkhotakota Wildlife Park

- **38** .... opportunities

- a reduction in the number of poachers and **39** ....

- an example of conservation that other parks can follow

- an increase in **40** .... as a contributor to GDP

READING

READING PASSAGE 1

*You should spend about 20 minutes on **Questions 1–13**, which are based on Reading Passage 1 below.*

Urban farming

In Paris, urban farmers are trying a soil-free approach to agriculture that uses less space and fewer resources. Could it help cities face the threats to our food supplies?

On top of a striking new exhibition hall in southern Paris, the world's largest urban rooftop farm has started to bear fruit. Strawberries that are small, intensely flavoured and resplendently red sprout abundantly from large plastic tubes. Peer inside and you see the tubes are completely hollow, the roots of dozens of strawberry plants dangling down inside them. From identical vertical tubes nearby burst row upon row of lettuces; near those are aromatic herbs, such as basil, sage and peppermint. Opposite, in narrow, horizontal trays packed not with soil but with coconut fibre, grow cherry tomatoes, shiny aubergines and brightly coloured chards.

Pascal Hardy, an engineer and sustainable development consultant, began experimenting with vertical farming and aeroponic growing towers – as the soil-free plastic tubes are known – on his Paris apartment block roof five years ago. The urban rooftop space above the exhibition hall is somewhat bigger: 14,000 square metres and almost exactly the size of a couple of football pitches. Already, the team of young urban farmers who tend it have picked, in one day, 3,000 lettuces and 150 punnets of strawberries. When the remaining two thirds of the vast open area are in production, 20 staff will harvest up to 1,000 kg of perhaps 35 different varieties of fruit and vegetables, every day. 'We're not ever, obviously, going to feed the whole city this way,' cautions Hardy. 'In the urban environment you're working with very significant practical constraints, clearly, on what you can do and where. But if enough unused space can be developed like this, there's no reason why you shouldn't eventually target maybe between 5% and 10% of consumption.'

Perhaps most significantly, however, this is a real-life showcase for the work of Hardy's flourishing urban agriculture consultancy, Agripolis, which is currently fielding enquiries from around the world to design, build and equip a new breed of soil-free inner-city farm. 'The method's advantages are many,' he says. 'First, I don't much like the fact that most of the fruit and vegetables we eat have been treated with something like 17 different pesticides, or that the intensive farming techniques that produced them are such huge generators of greenhouse gases. I don't much like the fact, either, that they've travelled an average of 2,000 refrigerated kilometres to my plate, that their quality is so poor, because the varieties are selected for their capacity to withstand such substantial journeys, or that 80% of the price I pay goes to wholesalers and transport companies, not the producers.'

Produce grown using this soil-free method, on the other hand – which relies solely on a small quantity of water, enriched with organic nutrients, pumped around a closed circuit of pipes, towers and trays – is 'produced up here, and sold locally, just down there. It barely travels at all,' Hardy says. 'You can select crop varieties for their flavour, not their resistance to the transport and storage chain, and you can pick them when they're really at their best, and not before.' No soil is exhausted, and the water that gently showers the plants' roots every 12 minutes is recycled, so the method uses 90% less water than a classic intensive farm for the same yield.

Urban farming is not, of course, a new phenomenon. Inner-city agriculture is booming from Shanghai to Detroit and Tokyo to Bangkok. Strawberries are being grown in disused shipping containers, mushrooms in underground carparks. Aeroponic farming, he says, is 'virtuous'. The equipment weighs little, can be installed on almost any flat surface and is cheap to buy: roughly €100 to €150 per square metre. It is cheap to run, too, consuming a tiny fraction of the electricity used by some techniques.

Produce grown this way typically sells at prices that, while generally higher than those of classic intensive agriculture, are lower than soil-based organic growers. There are limits to what farmers can grow this way, of course, and much of the produce is suited to the summer months. 'Root vegetables we cannot do, at least not yet,' he says. 'Radishes are OK, but carrots, potatoes, that kind of thing – the roots are simply too long. Fruit trees are obviously not an option. And beans tend to take up a lot of space for not much return.' Nevertheless, urban farming of the kind being practised in Paris is one part of a bigger and fast-changing picture that is bringing food production closer to our lives.

Test 1

Questions 1–3

Complete the sentences below.

*Choose **NO MORE THAN TWO WORDS AND/OR A NUMBER** from the passage for each answer.*

Write your answers in boxes 1–3 on your answer sheet.

Urban farming in Paris

1 Vertical tubes are used to grow strawberries, ... and herbs.

2 There will eventually be a daily harvest of as much as .... in weight of fruit and vegetables.

3 It may be possible that the farm's produce will account for as much as 10% of the city's .... overall.

Questions 4–7

Complete the table below.

*Choose **ONE WORD ONLY** from the passage for each answer.*

Write your answers in boxes 4–7 on your answer sheet.

Intensive farming versus aeroponic urban farming			
	Growth	**Selection**	**Sale**
Intensive farming	• wide range of **4** .... used • techniques pollute air	• quality not good • varieties of fruit and vegetables chosen that can survive long **5**	• **6** .... receive very little of overall income
Aeroponic urban farming	• no soil used • nutrients added to water, which is recycled	• produce chosen because of its **7**	

Questions 8–13

Do the following statements agree with the information given in Reading Passage 1?

In boxes 8–13 on your answer sheet, write

> **TRUE**   *if the statement agrees with the information*
> **FALSE**   *if the statement contradicts the information*
> **NOT GIVEN** *if there is no information on this*

8   Urban farming can take place above or below ground.

9   Some of the equipment used in aeroponic farming can be made by hand.

10 Urban farming relies more on electricity than some other types of farming.

11 Fruit and vegetables grown on an aeroponic urban farm are cheaper than traditionally grown organic produce.

12 Most produce can be grown on an aeroponic urban farm at any time of the year.

13 Beans take longer to grow on an urban farm than other vegetables.

→ p. 120

READING PASSAGE 2

*You should spend about 20 minutes on **Questions 14–26**, which are based on Reading Passage 2 below.*

Forest management in Pennsylvania, USA

How managing low-quality wood (also known as low-use wood) for bioenergy can encourage sustainable forest management

A A tree's 'value' depends on several factors including its species, size, form, condition, quality, function, and accessibility, and depends on the management goals for a given forest. The same tree can be valued very differently by each person who looks at it. A large, straight black cherry tree has high value as timber to be cut into logs or made into furniture, but for a landowner more interested in wildlife habitat, the real value of that stem (or trunk) may be the food it provides to animals. Likewise, if the tree suffers from black knot disease, its value for timber decreases, but to a woodworker interested in making bowls, it brings an opportunity for a unique and beautiful piece of art.

B In the past, Pennsylvania landowners were solely interested in the value of their trees as high-quality timber. The norm was to remove the stems of highest quality and leave behind poorly formed trees that were not as well suited to the site where they grew. This practice, called 'high-grading', has left a legacy of 'low-use wood' in the forests. Some people even call these 'junk trees', and they are abundant in Pennsylvania. These trees have lower economic value for traditional timber markets, compete for growth with higher-value trees, shade out desirable regeneration and decrease the health of a stand* leaving it more vulnerable to poor weather and disease. Management that specifically targets low-use wood can help landowners manage these forest health issues, and wood energy markets help promote this.

C Wood energy markets can accept less expensive wood material of lower quality than would be suitable for traditional timber markets. Most wood used for energy in Pennsylvania is used to produce heat or electricity through combustion. Many schools and hospitals use wood boiler systems to heat and power their facilities, many homes are primarily heated with wood, and some coal plants incorporate wood into their coal streams to produce electricity. Wood can also be gasified for electrical generation and can even be made into liquid fuels like ethanol and gasoline for lorries and cars. All these products are made primarily from low-use wood. Several tree- and plant-cutting approaches, which could greatly improve the long-term quality of a forest, focus strongly or solely on the use of wood for those markets.

---

* Stand – An area covered with trees that have common features (e.g. size)

D   One such approach is called a Timber Stand Improvement (TSI) Cut. In a TSI Cut, really poor-quality tree and plant material is cut down to allow more space, light, and other resources to the highest-valued stems that remain. Removing invasive plants might be another primary goal of a TSI Cut. The stems that are left behind might then grow in size and develop more foliage and larger crowns or tops that produce more coverage for wildlife; they have a better chance to regenerate in a less crowded environment. TSI Cuts can be tailored to one farmer's specific management goals for his or her land.

E   Another approach that might yield a high amount of low-use wood is a Salvage Cut. With the many pests and pathogens visiting forests including hemlock wooly adelgid, Asian longhorned beetle, emerald ash borer, and gypsy moth, to name just a few, it is important to remember that those working in the forests can help ease these issues through cutting procedures. These types of cut reduce the number of sick trees and seek to manage the future spread of a pest problem. They leave vigorous trees that have stayed healthy enough to survive the outbreak.

F   A Shelterwood Cut, which only takes place in a mature forest that has already been thinned several times, involves removing all the mature trees when other seedlings have become established. This then allows the forester to decide which tree species are regenerated. It leaves a young forest where all trees are at a similar point in their growth. It can also be used to develop a two-tier forest so that there are two harvests and the money that comes in is spread out over a decade or more.

G   Thinnings and dense and dead wood removal for fire prevention also center on the production of low-use wood. However, it is important to remember that some retention of what many would classify as low-use wood is very important. The tops of trees that have been cut down should be left on the site so that their nutrients cycle back into the soil. In addition, trees with many cavities are extremely important habitats for insect predators like woodpeckers, bats and small mammals. They help control problem insects and increase the health and resilience of the forest. It is also important to remember that not all small trees are low-use. For example, many species like hawthorn provide food for wildlife. Finally, rare species of trees in a forest should also stay behind as they add to its structural diversity.

Questions 14–18

Reading Passage 2 has seven paragraphs, **A–G**.

Which paragraph contains the following information?

*Write the correct letter, **A–G**, in boxes 14–18 on your answer sheet.*

NB *You may use any letter more than once.*

14 bad outcomes for a forest when people focus only on its financial reward

15 reference to the aspects of any tree that contribute to its worth

16 mention of the potential use of wood to help run vehicles

17 examples of insects that attack trees

18 an alternative name for trees that produce low-use wood

Questions 19–21

Look at the following purposes (Questions 19–21) and the list of timber cuts below.

*Match each purpose with the correct timber cut, **A**, **B** or **C**.*

*Write the correct letter, **A**, **B** or **C**, in boxes 19–21 on your answer sheet.*

NB *You may use any letter more than once.*

19   to remove trees that are diseased

20   to generate income across a number of years

21   to create a forest whose trees are close in age

List of Timber Cuts

A   a TSI Cut

B   a Salvage Cut

C   a Shelterwood Cut

Questions 22–26

Complete the sentences below.

*Choose **ONE WORD ONLY** from the passage for each answer.*

Write your answers in boxes 22–26 on your answer sheet.

22   Some dead wood is removed to avoid the possibility of ………… .

23   The ………… from the tops of cut trees can help improve soil quality.

24   Some damaged trees should be left, as their ………… provide habitats for a range of creatures.

25   Some trees that are small, such as ………… , are a source of food for animals and insects.

26   Any trees that are ………… should be left to grow, as they add to the variety of species in the forest.

READING PASSAGE 3

*You should spend about 20 minutes on **Questions 27–40**, which are based on Reading Passage 3 below.*

Conquering Earth's space junk problem

Satellites, rocket shards and collision debris are creating major traffic risks in orbit around the planet. Researchers are working to reduce these threats

A   Last year, commercial companies, military and civil departments and amateurs sent more than 400 satellites into orbit, over four times the yearly average in the previous decade. Numbers could rise even more sharply if leading space companies follow through on plans to deploy hundreds to thousands of large constellations of satellites to space in the next few years.

All that traffic can lead to disaster. Ten years ago, a US commercial Iridium satellite smashed into an inactive Russian communications satellite called Cosmos-2251, creating thousands of new pieces of space shrapnel that now threaten other satellites in low Earth orbit – the zone stretching up to 2,000 kilometres in altitude. Altogether, there are roughly 20,000 human-made objects in orbit, from working satellites to small rocket pieces. And satellite operators can't steer away from every potential crash, because each move consumes time and fuel that could otherwise be used for the spacecraft's main job.

B   Concern about space junk goes back to the beginning of the satellite era, but the number of objects in orbit is rising so rapidly that researchers are investigating new ways of attacking the problem. Several teams are trying to improve methods for assessing what is in orbit, so that satellite operators can work more efficiently in ever-more-crowded space. Some researchers are now starting to compile a massive data set that includes the best possible information on where everything is in orbit. Others are developing taxonomies of space debris – working on measuring properties such as the shape and size of an object, so that satellite operators know how much to worry about what's coming their way.

The alternative, many say, is unthinkable. Just a few uncontrolled space crashes could generate enough debris to set off a runaway cascade of fragments, rendering near-Earth space unusable. 'If we go on like this, we will reach a point of no return,' says Carolin Frueh, an astrodynamical researcher at Purdue University in West Lafayette, Indiana.

C   Even as our ability to monitor space objects increases, so too does the total number of items in orbit. That means companies, governments and other players in space are collaborating in new ways to avoid a shared threat. International groups such as the Inter-Agency Space Debris Coordination Committee have developed guidelines on space sustainability. Those include inactivating satellites at the end of their useful life by venting pressurised materials or leftover fuel that might lead to explosions. The intergovernmental groups also advise lowering satellites deep enough into the atmosphere that they will burn up or disintegrate within 25 years. But so far, only about half of all missions have abided by this 25-year goal, says Holger Krag, head of the European Space Agency's space-debris office in Darmstadt, Germany. Operators of the planned large constellations of satellites say they will be responsible stewards in their enterprises in space, but Krag worries that problems could increase, despite their best intentions. 'What happens to those that fail or go bankrupt?' he asks. 'They are probably not going to spend money to remove their satellites from space.'

D   In theory, given the vastness of space, satellite operators should have plenty of room for all these missions to fly safely without ever nearing another object. So some scientists are tackling the problem of space junk by trying to find out where all the debris is to a high degree of precision. That would alleviate the need for many of the unnecessary manoeuvres that are carried out to avoid potential collisions. 'If you knew precisely where everything was, you would almost never have a problem,' says Marlon Sorge, a space-debris specialist at the Aerospace Corporation in El Segundo, California.

E   The field is called space traffic management, because it's similar to managing traffic on the roads or in the air. Think about a busy day at an airport, says Moriba Jah, an astrodynamicist at the University of Texas at Austin: planes line up in the sky, landing and taking off close to one another in a carefully choreographed routine. Air-traffic controllers know the location of the planes down to one metre in accuracy. The same can't be said for space debris. Not all objects in orbit are known, and even those included in databases are not tracked consistently.

F   An additional problem is that there is no authoritative catalogue that accurately lists the orbits of all known space debris. Jah illustrates this with a web-based database that he has developed. It draws on several sources, such as catalogues maintained by the US and Russian governments, to visualise where objects are in space. When he types in an identifier for a particular space object, the database draws a purple line to designate its orbit. Only this doesn't quite work for a number of objects, such as a Russian rocket body designated in the database as object number 32280. When Jah enters that number, the database draws two purple lines: the US and Russian sources contain two completely different orbits for the same object. Jah says that it is almost impossible to tell which is correct, unless a third source of information made it possible to cross-correlate.

Jah describes himself as a space environmentalist: 'I want to make space a place that is safe to operate, that is free and useful for generations to come.' Until that happens, he argues, the space community will continue devolving into a tragedy in which all spaceflight operators are polluting a common resource.

Questions 27–31

Reading Passage 3 has six sections, **A–F**.

Which section contains the following information?

*Write the correct letter, **A–F**, in boxes 27–31 on your answer sheet.*

27   a reference to the cooperation that takes place to try and minimise risk

28   an explanation of a person's aims

29   a description of a major collision that occurred in space

30   a comparison between tracking objects in space and the efficiency of a
transportation system

31   a reference to efforts to classify space junk

Questions 32–35

Complete the summary below.

*Choose **ONE WORD ONLY** from the passage for each answer.*

Write your answers in boxes 32–35 on your answer sheet.

The Inter-Agency Space Debris Coordination Committee

The committee gives advice on how the **32** .... of space can be
achieved. The committee advises that when satellites are no longer active, any
unused **33** .... or pressurised material that could cause
34 .... should be removed.

Although operators of large satellite constellations accept that they have obligations
as stewards of space, Holger Krag points out that the operators that become
35 .... are unlikely to prioritise removing their satellites from space.

Questions 36–40

Look at the following statements (Questions 36–40) and the list of people below.

*Match each statement with the correct person, **A**, **B**, **C** or **D**.*

*Write the correct letter, **A**, **B**, **C** or **D**, in boxes 36–40 on your answer sheet.*

NB *You may use any letter more than once.*

36 Knowing the exact location of space junk would help prevent any possible danger.

37 Space should be available to everyone and should be preserved for the future.

38 A recommendation regarding satellites is widely ignored.

39 There is conflicting information about where some satellites are in space.

40 There is a risk we will not be able to undo the damage that occurs in space.

List of People
A Carolin Frueh
B Holger Krag
C Marlon Sorge
D Moriba Jah

WRITING TASK 1

You should spend about 20 minutes on this task.

The graph below gives information about the percentage of the population in four Asian countries living in cities from 1970 to 2020, with predictions for 2030 and 2040.

Summarise the information by selecting and reporting the main features, and make comparisons where relevant.

Write at least 150 words.

Percentage of the population living in cities

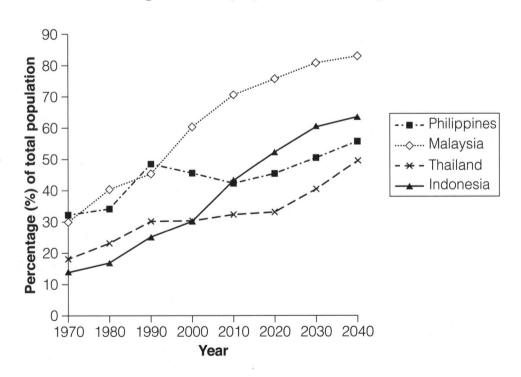

WRITING TASK 2

You should spend about 40 minutes on this task.

Write about the following topic:

The most important aim of science should be to improve people's lives.

To what extent do you agree or disagree with this statement?

Give reasons for your answer and include any relevant examples from your own knowledge or experience.

Write at least 250 words.

SPEAKING

PART 1

The examiner asks you about yourself, your home, work or studies and other familiar topics.

Example Speaking test video

EXAMPLE

Paying bills

- What kinds of bills do you have to pay?
- How do you usually pay your bills – in cash or by another method? [Why?]
- Have you ever forgotten to pay a bill? [Why/Why not?]
- Is there anything you could do to make your bills cheaper? [Why/Why not?]

PART 2

Describe some food or drink that you learned to prepare.

You should say:
> **what food or drink you learned to prepare**
> **when and where you learned to prepare this**
> **how you learned to prepare this**

and explain how you felt about learning to prepare this food or drink.

You will have to talk about the topic for one to two minutes. You have one minute to think about what you are going to say. You can make some notes to help you if you wish.

PART 3

Discussion topics:

Young people and cooking

Example questions:
What kinds of things can children learn to cook?
Do you think it is important for children to learn to cook?
Do you think young people should learn to cook at home or at school?

Working as a chef

Example questions:
How enjoyable do you think it would be to work as a professional chef?
What skills does a person need to be a great chef?
How much influence do celebrity/TV chefs have on what ordinary people cook?

Test 2

PART 1   Questions 1–10

Questions 1–5

Complete the notes below.

*Write **ONE WORD ONLY** for each answer.*

Listening test audio

Working at Milo's Restaurants

Benefits

- 1 .... provided for all staff
- 2 .... during weekdays at all Milo's Restaurants
- 3 .... provided after midnight

Person specification

- must be prepared to work well in a team
- must care about maintaining a high standard of 4 ....
- must have a qualification in 5 ....

Questions 6–10

Complete the table below.

Write ONE WORD AND/OR A NUMBER for each answer.

Location	Job title	Responsibilities include	Pay and conditions
6 .... Street	Breakfast supervisor	Checking portions, etc. are correct Making sure 7 .... is clean	Starting salary 8 £ .... per hour Start work at 5.30 a.m.
City Road	Junior chef	Supporting senior chefs Maintaining stock and organising 9	Annual salary £23,000 No work on a 10 .... once a month

PART 2   *Questions 11–20*

Questions 11 and 12

*Choose **TWO** letters, **A–E**.*

Listening test audio

What are the **TWO** main reasons why this site has been chosen for the housing development?

    A   It has suitable geographical features.
    B   There is easy access to local facilities.
    C   It has good connections with the airport.
    D   The land is of little agricultural value.
    E   It will be convenient for workers.

Questions 13 and 14

*Choose **TWO** letters, **A–E**.*

Which **TWO** aspects of the planned housing development have people given positive feedback about?

    A   the facilities for cyclists
    B   the impact on the environment
    C   the encouragement of good relations between residents
    D   the low cost of all the accommodation
    E   the rural location

Questions 15–20

Label the map below.

*Write the correct letter, **A–I**, next to Questions 15–20.*

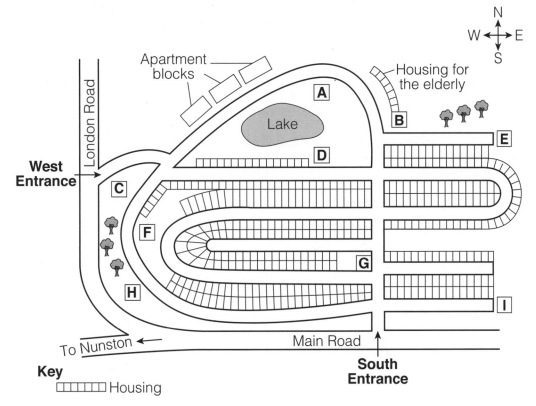

Key
▭▭▭▭ Housing

15	School	....
16	Sports centre	....
17	Clinic	....
18	Community centre	....
19	Supermarket	....
20	Playground	....

PART 3   *Questions 21–30*

Questions 21–24

Listening test audio

*Choose the correct letter, **A**, **B** or **C**.*

21   Why do the students think the Laki eruption of 1783 is so important?

    A   It was the most severe eruption in modern times.
    B   It led to the formal study of volcanoes.
    C   It had a profound effect on society.

22   What surprised Adam about observations made at the time?

    A   the number of places producing them
    B   the contradictions in them
    C   the lack of scientific data to support them

23   According to Michelle, what did the contemporary sources say about the Laki haze?

    A   People thought it was similar to ordinary fog.
    B   It was associated with health issues.
    C   It completely blocked out the sun for weeks.

24   Adam corrects Michelle when she claims that Benjamin Franklin

    A   came to the wrong conclusion about the cause of the haze.
    B   was the first to identify the reason for the haze.
    C   supported the opinions of other observers about the haze.

Questions 25 and 26

*Choose **TWO** letters, **A–E**.*

Which **TWO** issues following the Laki eruption surprised the students?

    A   how widespread the effects were
    B   how long-lasting the effects were
    C   the number of deaths it caused
    D   the speed at which the volcanic ash cloud spread
    E   how people ignored the warning signs

Questions 27–30

What comment do the students make about the impact of the Laki eruption on the following countries?

*Choose **FOUR** answers from the box and write the correct letter, **A–F**, next to Questions 27–30.*

Comments
A   This country suffered the most severe loss of life.
B   The impact on agriculture was predictable.
C   There was a significant increase in deaths of young people.
D   Animals suffered from a sickness.
E   This country saw the highest rise in food prices in the world.
F   It caused a particularly harsh winter.

Countries

27   Iceland   ....

28   Egypt   ....

29   UK   ....

30   USA   ....

PART 4   *Questions 31–40*

Complete the notes below.

Write ONE WORD ONLY for each answer.

Listening test audio

Pockets

Reason for choice of subject

- They are **31** .... but can be overlooked by consumers and designers.

Pockets in men's clothes

- Men started to wear **32** .... in the 18th century.

- A **33** .... sewed pockets into the lining of the garments.

- The wearer could use the pockets for small items.

- Bigger pockets might be made for men who belonged to a certain type of **34** ....

Pockets in women's clothes

- Women's pockets were less **35** .... than men's.

- Women were very concerned about pickpockets.

- Pockets were produced in pairs using **36** .... to link them together.

- Pockets hung from the women's **37** .... under skirts and petticoats.

- Items such as **38** .... could be reached through a gap in the material.

- Pockets, of various sizes, stayed inside clothing for many decades.

- When dresses changed shape, hidden pockets had a negative effect on the **39** .... of women.

- Bags called 'pouches' became popular, before women carried a **40** ....

 → 🔊 p. 121 📄 p. 108

READING PASSAGE 1

*You should spend about 20 minutes on **Questions 1–13**, which are based on Reading Passage 1 below.*

Stonehenge

For centuries, historians and archaeologists have puzzled over the many mysteries of Stonehenge, a prehistoric monument that took an estimated 1,500 years to erect. Located on Salisbury Plain in southern England, it is comprised of roughly 100 massive upright stones placed in a circular layout.

Archaeologists believe England's most iconic prehistoric ruin was built in several stages, with the earliest constructed 5,000 or more years ago. First, Neolithic* Britons used primitive tools, which may have been fashioned out of deer antlers, to dig a massive circular ditch and bank, or henge. Deep pits dating back to that era and located within the circle may have once held a ring of timber posts, according to some scholars.

Several hundred years later, it is thought, Stonehenge's builders hoisted an estimated 80 bluestones, 43 of which remain today, into standing positions and placed them in either a horseshoe or circular formation. These stones have been traced all the way to the Preseli Hills in Wales, some 300 kilometres from Stonehenge. How, then, did prehistoric builders without sophisticated tools or engineering haul these boulders, which weigh up to four tons, over such a great distance?

According to one long-standing theory among archaeologists, Stonehenge's builders fashioned sledges and rollers out of tree trunks to lug the bluestones from the Preseli Hills. They then transferred the boulders onto rafts and floated them first along the Welsh coast and then up the River Avon toward Salisbury Plain; alternatively, they may have towed each stone with a fleet of vessels. More recent archaeological hypotheses have them transporting the bluestones with supersized wicker baskets on a combination of ball bearings and long grooved planks, hauled by oxen.

As early as the 1970s, geologists have been adding their voices to the debate over how Stonehenge came into being. Challenging the classic image of industrious builders pushing, carting, rolling or hauling giant stones from faraway Wales, some scientists have suggested that it was glaciers, not humans, that carried the bluestones to Salisbury Plain. Most archaeologists have remained sceptical about this theory, however, wondering how the forces of nature could possibly have delivered the exact number of stones needed to complete the circle.

---

* Neolithic – The era, also known as the New Stone Age, which began around 12,000 years ago and ended around 3500 BCE

The third phase of construction took place around 2000 BCE. At this point, sandstone slabs – known as 'sarsens' – were arranged into an outer crescent or ring; some were assembled into the iconic three-pieced structures called trilithons that stand tall in the centre of Stonehenge. Some 50 of these stones are now visible on the site, which may once have contained many more. Radiocarbon dating has revealed that work continued at Stonehenge until roughly 1600 BCE, with the bluestones in particular being repositioned multiple times.

But who were the builders of Stonehenge? In the 17th century, archaeologist John Aubrey made the claim that Stonehenge was the work of druids, who had important religious, judicial and political roles in Celtic[**] society. This theory was widely popularized by the antiquarian William Stukeley, who had unearthed primitive graves at the site. Even today, people who identify as modern druids continue to gather at Stonehenge for the summer solstice. However, in the mid-20th century, radiocarbon dating demonstrated that Stonehenge stood more than 1,000 years before the Celts inhabited the region.

Many modern historians and archaeologists now agree that several distinct tribes of people contributed to Stonehenge, each undertaking a different phase of its construction. Bones, tools and other artefacts found on the site seem to support this hypothesis. The first stage was achieved by Neolithic agrarians who were likely to have been indigenous to the British Isles. Later, it is believed, groups with advanced tools and a more communal way of life left their mark on the site. Some believe that they were immigrants from the European continent, while others maintain that they were probably native Britons, descended from the original builders.

If the facts surrounding the architects and construction of Stonehenge remain shadowy at best, the purpose of the striking monument is even more of a mystery. While there is consensus among the majority of modern scholars that Stonehenge once served the function of burial ground, they have yet to determine what other purposes it had.

In the 1960s, the astronomer Gerald Hawkins suggested that the cluster of megalithic stones operated as a form of calendar, with different points corresponding to astrological phenomena such as solstices, equinoxes and eclipses occurring at different times of the year. While his theory has received a considerable amount of attention over the decades, critics maintain that Stonehenge's builders probably lacked the knowledge necessary to predict such events or that England's dense cloud cover would have obscured their view of the skies.

More recently, signs of illness and injury in the human remains unearthed at Stonehenge led a group of British archaeologists to speculate that it was considered a place of healing, perhaps because bluestones were thought to have curative powers.

[**] Celtic – The Celts were people who lived in Britain and northwest Europe during the Iron Age from 600 BCE to 43 CE

Questions 1–8

Complete the notes below.

*Choose **NO MORE THAN TWO WORDS** from the passage for each answer.*

Write your answers in boxes 1–8 on your answer sheet.

Stonehenge

Construction

Stage 1:

• the ditch and henge were dug, possibly using tools made from **1** ....

• **2** .... may have been arranged in deep pits inside the circle

Stage 2:

• bluestones from the Preseli Hills were placed in standing position

• theories about the transportation of the bluestones:

   – archaeological:

      o builders used **3** .... to make sledges and rollers

      o **4** .... pulled them on giant baskets

   – geological:

      o they were brought from Wales by **5** ....

Stage 3:

• sandstone slabs were arranged into an outer crescent or ring

Builders

• a theory arose in the 17th century that its builders were Celtic **6** ....

Purpose

• many experts agree it has been used as a **7** .... site

• in the 1960s, it was suggested that it worked as a kind of **8** ....

Questions 9–13

Do the following statements agree with the information given in Reading Passage 1?

In boxes 9–13 on your answer sheet, write

> **TRUE**   *if the statement agrees with the information*
> **FALSE**   *if the statement contradicts the information*
> **NOT GIVEN**   *if there is no information on this*

9   During the third phase of construction, sandstone slabs were placed in both the outer areas and the middle of the Stonehenge site.

10 There is scientific proof that the bluestones stood in the same spot until approximately 1600 BCE.

11 John Aubrey's claim about Stonehenge was supported by 20th-century findings.

12 Objects discovered at Stonehenge seem to indicate that it was constructed by a number of different groups of people.

13 Criticism of Gerald Hawkins' theory about Stonehenge has come mainly from other astronomers.

READING PASSAGE 2

*You should spend about 20 minutes on **Questions 14–26**, which are based on Reading Passage 2 below.*

Living with artificial intelligence

Powerful artificial intelligence (AI) needs to be reliably aligned with human values, but does this mean AI will eventually have to police those values?

This has been the decade of AI, with one astonishing feat after another. A chess-playing AI that can defeat not only all human chess players, but also all previous human-programmed chess machines, after learning the game in just four hours? That's yesterday's news, what's next? True, these prodigious accomplishments are all in so-called narrow AI, where machines perform highly specialised tasks. But many experts believe this restriction is very temporary. By mid-century, we may have artificial general intelligence (AGI) – machines that can achieve human-level performance on the full range of tasks that we ourselves can tackle.

If so, there's little reason to think it will stop there. Machines will be free of many of the physical constraints on human intelligence. Our brains run at slow biochemical processing speeds on the power of a light bulb, and their size is restricted by the dimensions of the human birth canal. It is remarkable what they accomplish, given these handicaps. But they may be as far from the physical limits of thought as our eyes are from the incredibly powerful Webb Space Telescope.

Once machines are better than us at designing even smarter machines, progress towards these limits could accelerate. What would this mean for us? Could we ensure a safe and worthwhile coexistence with such machines? On the plus side, AI is already useful and profitable for many things, and super AI might be expected to be super useful, and super profitable. But the more powerful AI becomes, the more important it will be to specify its goals with great care. Folklore is full of tales of people who ask for the wrong thing, with disastrous consequences – King Midas, for example, might have wished that everything he touched turned to gold, but didn't really intend this to apply to his breakfast.

So we need to create powerful AI machines that are 'human-friendly' – that have goals reliably aligned with our own values. One thing that makes this task difficult is that we are far from reliably human-friendly ourselves. We do many terrible things to each other and to many other creatures with whom we share the planet. If superintelligent machines don't do a lot better than us, we'll be in deep trouble. We'll have powerful new intelligence amplifying the dark sides of our own fallible natures.

For safety's sake, then, we want the machines to be ethically as well as cognitively superhuman. We want them to aim for the moral high ground, not for the troughs in which many of us spend some of our time. Luckily they'll be smart enough for the job. If there are routes to the moral high ground, they'll be better than us at finding them, and steering us in the right direction.

However, there are two big problems with this utopian vision. One is how we get the machines started on the journey, the other is what it would mean to reach this destination. The 'getting started' problem is that we need to tell the machines what they're looking for with sufficient clarity that we can be confident they will find it – whatever 'it' actually turns out to be. This won't be easy, given that we are tribal creatures and conflicted about the ideals ourselves. We often ignore the suffering of strangers, and even contribute to it, at least indirectly. How then, do we point machines in the direction of something better?

As for the 'destination' problem, we might, by putting ourselves in the hands of these moral guides and gatekeepers, be sacrificing our own autonomy – an important part of what makes us human. Machines who are better than us at sticking to the moral high ground may be expected to discourage some of the lapses we presently take for granted. We might lose our freedom to discriminate in favour of our own communities, for example.

Loss of freedom to behave badly isn't always a bad thing, of course: denying ourselves the freedom to put children to work in factories, or to smoke in restaurants are signs of progress. But are we ready for ethical silicon police limiting our options? They might be so good at doing it that we won't notice them; but few of us are likely to welcome such a future.

These issues might seem far-fetched, but they are to some extent already here. AI already has some input into how resources are used in our National Health Service (NHS) here in the UK, for example. If it was given a greater role, it might do so much more efficiently than humans can manage, and act in the interests of taxpayers and those who use the health system. However, we'd be depriving some humans (e.g. senior doctors) of the control they presently enjoy. Since we'd want to ensure that people are treated equally and that policies are fair, the goals of AI would need to be specified correctly.

We have a new powerful technology to deal with – itself, literally, a new way of thinking. For our own safety, we need to point these new thinkers in the right direction, and get them to act well for us. It is not yet clear whether this is possible, but if it is, it will require a cooperative spirit, and a willingness to set aside self-interest.

Both general intelligence and moral reasoning are often thought to be uniquely human capacities. But safety seems to require that we think of them as a package: if we are to give general intelligence to machines, we'll need to give them moral authority, too. And where exactly would that leave human beings? All the more reason to think about the destination now, and to be careful about what we wish for.

Questions 14–19

*Choose the correct letter, **A**, **B**, **C** or **D**.*

Write the correct letter in boxes 14–19 on your answer sheet.

14 What point does the writer make about AI in the first paragraph?

    A   It is difficult to predict how quickly AI will progress.
    B   Much can be learned about the use of AI in chess machines.
    C   The future is unlikely to see limitations on the capabilities of AI.
    D   Experts disagree on which specialised tasks AI will be able to perform.

15 What is the writer doing in the second paragraph?

    A   explaining why machines will be able to outperform humans
    B   describing the characteristics that humans and machines share
    C   giving information about the development of machine intelligence
    D   indicating which aspects of humans are the most advanced

16 Why does the writer mention the story of King Midas?

    A   to compare different visions of progress
    B   to illustrate that poorly defined objectives can go wrong
    C   to emphasise the need for cooperation
    D   to point out the financial advantages of a course of action

17 What challenge does the writer refer to in the fourth paragraph?

    A   encouraging humans to behave in a more principled way
    B   deciding which values we want AI to share with us
    C   creating a better world for all creatures on the planet
    D   ensuring AI is more human-friendly than we are ourselves

18 What does the writer suggest about the future of AI in the fifth paragraph?

    A   The safety of machines will become a key issue.
    B   It is hard to know what impact machines will have on the world.
    C   Machines will be superior to humans in certain respects.
    D   Many humans will oppose machines having a wider role.

19 Which of the following best summarises the writer's argument in the sixth paragraph?

    A   More intelligent machines will result in greater abuses of power.
    B   Machine learning will share very few features with human learning.
    C   There are a limited number of people with the knowledge to program machines.
    D   Human shortcomings will make creating the machines we need more difficult.

Questions 20–23

Do the following statements agree with the claims of the writer in Reading Passage 2?

In boxes 20–23 on your answer sheet, write

> **YES**   *if the statement agrees with the claims of the writer*
> **NO**   *if the statement contradicts the claims of the writer*
> **NOT GIVEN** *if it is impossible to say what the writer thinks about this*

20   Machines with the ability to make moral decisions may prevent us from promoting the interests of our communities.

21   Silicon police would need to exist in large numbers in order to be effective.

22   Many people are comfortable with the prospect of their independence being restricted by machines.

23   If we want to ensure that machines act in our best interests, we all need to work together.

Questions 24–26

*Complete the summary using the list of phrases, **A–F**, below.*

*Write the correct letter, **A–F**, in boxes 24–26 on your answer sheet.*

Using AI in the UK health system

AI currently has a limited role in the way **24** .... are allocated in the health service. The positive aspect of AI having a bigger role is that it would be more efficient and lead to patient benefits. However, such a change would result, for example, in certain **25** .... not having their current level of **26** .... It is therefore important that AI goals are appropriate so that discriminatory practices could be avoided.

A medical practitioners	**B** specialised tasks		**C** available resources
D reduced illness	**E** professional authority	**F** technology experts	

READING PASSAGE 3

*You should spend about 20 minutes on **Questions 27–40**, which are based on Reading Passage 3 below.*

An ideal city

Leonardo da Vinci's ideal city was centuries ahead of its time

The word 'genius' is universally associated with the name of Leonardo da Vinci. A true Renaissance man, he embodied scientific spirit, artistic talent and humanist sensibilities. Five hundred years have passed since Leonardo died in his home at Château du Clos Lucé, outside Tours, France. Yet far from fading into insignificance, his thinking has carried down the centuries and still surprises today.

The Renaissance marked the transition from the 15th century to modernity and took place after the spread of the plague in the 14th century, which caused a global crisis resulting in some 200 million deaths across Europe and Asia. Today, the world is on the cusp of a climate crisis, which is predicted to cause widespread displacement, extinctions and death, if left unaddressed. Then, as now, radical solutions were called for to revolutionise the way people lived and safeguard humanity against catastrophe.

Around 1486 – after a pestilence that killed half the population in Milan, Italy – Leonardo turned his thoughts to urban planning problems. Following a typical Renaissance trend, he began to work on an 'ideal city' project, which – due to its excessive costs – would remain unfulfilled. Yet given that unsustainable urban models are a key cause of global climate change today, it's only natural to wonder how Leonardo might have changed the shape of modern cities.

Although the Renaissance is renowned as an era of incredible progress in art and architecture, it is rarely noted that the 15th century also marked the birth of urbanism as a true academic discipline. The rigour and method behind the conscious conception of a city had been largely missing in Western thought until the moment when prominent Renaissance men pushed forward large-scale urban projects in Italy, such as the reconfiguration of the town of Pienza and the expansion of the city of Ferrara. These works surely inspired Leonardo's decision to rethink the design of medieval cities, with their winding and overcrowded streets and with houses piled against one another.

It is not easy to identify a coordinated vision of Leonardo's ideal city because of his disordered way of working with notes and sketches. But from the largest collection of Leonardo's papers ever assembled, a series of innovative thoughts can be reconstructed regarding the foundation of a new city along the Ticino River, which runs from Switzerland into Italy and is 248 kilometres long. He designed the city for the easy transport of goods and clean urban spaces, and he wanted a comfortable and spacious city, with well-ordered streets and architecture. He recommended 'high, strong walls', with 'towers and battlements of all necessary and pleasant beauty'.

His plans for a modern and 'rational' city were consistent with Renaissance ideals. But, in keeping with his personality, Leonardo included several innovations in his urban design. Leonardo wanted the city to be built on several levels, linked with vertical outdoor staircases. This design can be seen in some of today's high-rise buildings but was unconventional at the time. Indeed, this idea of taking full advantage of the interior spaces wasn't implemented until the 1920s and 1930s, with the birth of the Modernist movement.

While in the upper layers of the city, people could walk undisturbed between elegant palaces and streets, the lower layer was the place for services, trade, transport and industry. But the true originality of Leonardo's vision was its fusion of architecture and engineering. Leonardo designed extensive hydraulic plants to create artificial canals throughout the city. The canals, regulated by clocks and basins, were supposed to make it easier for boats to navigate inland. Leonardo also thought that the width of the streets ought to match the average height of the adjacent houses: a rule still followed in many contemporary cities across Italy, to allow access to sun and reduce the risk of damage from earthquakes.

Although some of these features existed in Roman cities, before Leonardo's drawings there had never been a multi-level, compact modern city which was thoroughly technically conceived. Indeed, it wasn't until the 19th century that some of his ideas were applied. For example, the subdivision of the city by function – with services and infrastructures located in the lower levels and wide and well-ventilated boulevards and walkways above for residents – is an idea that can be found in Georges-Eugène Haussmann's renovation of Paris under Emperor Napoleon III between 1853 and 1870.

Today, Leonardo's ideas are not simply valid, they actually suggest a way forward for urban planning. Many scholars think that the compact city, built upwards instead of outwards, integrated with nature (especially water systems), with efficient transport infrastructure, could help modern cities become more efficient and sustainable. This is yet another reason why Leonardo was aligned so closely with modern urban planning and centuries ahead of his time.

Questions 27–33

Do the following statements agree with the information given in Reading Passage 3?

In boxes 27–33 on your answer sheet, write

> **TRUE**   *if the statement agrees with the information*
> **FALSE**   *if the statement contradicts the information*
> **NOT GIVEN**   *if there is no information on this*

27 People first referred to Leonardo da Vinci as a genius 500 years ago.

28 The current climate crisis is predicted to cause more deaths than the plague.

29 Some of the challenges we face today can be compared to those of earlier times.

30 Leonardo da Vinci's 'ideal city' was constructed in the 15th century.

31 Poor town planning is a major contributor to climate change.

32 In Renaissance times, local people fought against the changes to Pienza and Ferrara.

33 Leonardo da Vinci kept a neat, organised record of his designs.

Questions 34–40

Complete the summary below.

*Choose **ONE WORD ONLY** from the passage for each answer.*

Write your answers in boxes 34–40 on your answer sheet.

Leonardo da Vinci's ideal city

A collection of Leonardo da Vinci's paperwork reveals his design of a new city beside the Ticino River. This was to provide better **34** .... for trade and a less polluted environment. Although Leonardo da Vinci's city shared many of the ideals of his time, some of his innovations were considered unconventional in their design. They included features that can be seen in some tower blocks today, such as **35** .... on the exterior of a building.

Leonardo da Vinci wasn't only an architect. His expertise in **36** .... was evident in his plans for artificial canals within his ideal city. He also believed that the height of houses should relate to the width of streets in case earthquakes occurred. The design of many cities in Italy today follows this **37** ....

While some cities from **38** .... times have aspects that can also be found in Leonardo's designs, his ideas weren't put into practice until long after his death. **39** .... is one example of a city that was redesigned in the 19th century in the way that Leonardo had envisaged. His ideas are also relevant to today's world, where building **40** .... no longer seems to be the best approach.

WRITING

WRITING TASK 1

You should spend about 20 minutes on this task.

The chart below shows the number of households in the US by their annual income in 2007, 2011 and 2015.

Summarise the information by selecting and reporting the main features, and make comparisons where relevant.

Write at least 150 words.

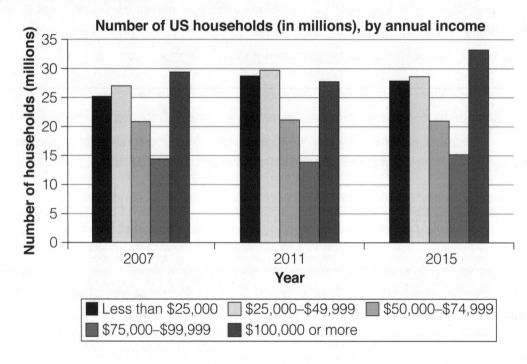

Number of US households (in millions), by annual income

WRITING TASK 2

You should spend about 40 minutes on this task.

Write about the following topic:

> *Some university students want to learn about other subjects in addition to their main subjects. Others believe it is more important to give all their time and attention to studying for a qualification.*
>
> *Discuss both these views and give your own opinion.*

Give reasons for your answer and include any relevant examples from your own knowledge or experience.

Write at least 250 words.

SPEAKING

PART 1

The examiner asks you about yourself, your home, work or studies and other familiar topics.

EXAMPLE

Science

- Did you like studying science when you were at school? [Why/Why not?]
- What do you remember about your science teachers at school?
- How interested are you in science now? [Why/Why not?]
- What do you think has been an important recent scientific development? [Why?]

PART 2

Describe a tourist attraction in your country that you would recommend.
 	
You should say:
    what the tourist attraction is
    where in your country this tourist attraction is
    what visitors can see and do at this tourist attraction
 	
and explain why you would recommend this tourist attraction.

You will have to talk about the topic for one to two minutes. You have one minute to think about what you are going to say. You can make some notes to help you if you wish.

PART 3

Discussion topics:

Museums and art galleries

Example questions:
What are the most popular museums and art galleries in … / where you live?
Do you believe that all museums and art galleries should be free?
What kinds of things make a museum or art gallery an interesting place to visit?

The holiday industry

Example questions:
Why, do you think, do some people book package holidays rather than travelling independently?
Would you say that large numbers of tourists cause problems for local people?
What sort of impact can large holiday resorts have on the environment?

Test 3

LISTENING

PART 1   Questions 1–10

Questions 1–4

Complete the form below.

Write **ONE WORD AND/OR A NUMBER** for each answer.

Listening test audio

Wayside Camera Club membership form	
Name:	Dan Green
Email address:	dan1068@market.com
Home address:	52 **1** .... Street, Peacetown
Heard about us:	from a **2** ....
Reasons for joining:	to enter competitions to **3** ....
Type of membership:	**4** .... membership (£30)

Questions 5–10

Complete the table below.

Write **NO MORE THAN TWO WORDS** for each answer.

Photography competitions		
Title of competition	**Instructions**	**Feedback to Dan**
5 ' .... '	A scene in the home	The picture's composition was not good.
'Beautiful Sunsets'	Scene must show some **6**	The **7** .... was wrong.
8 ' .... '	Scene must show **9**	The photograph was too **10** ....

→ 🔗 p. 123   📄 p. 109   55

PART 2   *Questions 11–20*

Listening test audio

Questions 11 and 12

*Choose **TWO** letters, **A–E**.*

Which **TWO** warnings does Dan give about picking mushrooms?

    A   Don't pick more than one variety of mushroom at a time.
    B   Don't pick mushrooms near busy roads.
    C   Don't eat mushrooms given to you.
    D   Don't eat mushrooms while picking them.
    E   Don't pick old mushrooms.

Questions 13 and 14

*Choose **TWO** letters, **A–E**.*

Which **TWO** ideas about wild mushrooms does Dan say are correct?

    A   Mushrooms should always be peeled before eating.
    B   Mushrooms eaten by animals may be unsafe.
    C   Cooking destroys toxins in mushrooms.
    D   Brightly coloured mushrooms can be edible.
    E   All poisonous mushrooms have a bad smell.

Questions 15–20

*Choose the correct letter, **A**, **B** or **C**.*

15 What advice does Dan give about picking mushrooms in parks?

    A   Choose wooded areas.
    B   Don't disturb wildlife.
    C   Get there early.

16 Dan says it is a good idea for beginners to

    A   use a mushroom app.
    B   join a group.
    C   take a reference book.

17 What does Dan say is important for conservation?

    A   selecting only fully grown mushrooms
    B   picking a limited amount of mushrooms
    C   avoiding areas where rare mushroom species grow

18 According to Dan, some varieties of wild mushrooms are in decline because there is

    A   a huge demand for them from restaurants.
    B   a lack of rain in this part of the country.
    C   a rise in building developments locally.

19 Dan says that when storing mushrooms, people should

    A   keep them in the fridge for no more than two days.
    B   keep them in a brown bag in a dark room.
    C   leave them for a period after washing them.

20 What does Dan say about trying new varieties of mushrooms?

    A   Experiment with different recipes.
    B   Expect some to have a strong taste.
    C   Cook them for a long time.

PART 3 *Questions 21–30*

Questions 21 and 22

Listening test audio

Choose TWO letters, A–E.

Which **TWO** opinions about the Luddites do the students express?

A   Their actions were ineffective.
B   They are still influential today.
C   They have received unfair criticism.
D   They were proved right.
E   Their attitude is understandable.

Questions 23 and 24

Choose TWO letters, A–E.

Which **TWO** predictions about the future of work are the students doubtful about?

A   Work will be more rewarding.
B   Unemployment will fall.
C   People will want to delay retiring.
D   Working hours will be shorter.
E   People will change jobs more frequently.

Questions 25–30

What comment do the students make about each of the following jobs?

*Choose **SIX** answers from the box and write the correct letter, **A–G**, next to Questions 25–30.*

Comments

A These jobs are likely to be at risk.

B Their role has become more interesting in recent years.

C The number of people working in this sector has fallen dramatically.

D This job will require more qualifications.

E Higher disposable income has led to a huge increase in jobs.

F There is likely to be a significant rise in demand for this service.

G Both employment and productivity have risen.

Jobs

25 Accountants   ....

26 Hairdressers   ....

27 Administrative staff   ....

28 Agricultural workers   ....

29 Care workers   ....

30 Bank clerks   ....

PART 4   *Questions 31–40*

Complete the notes below.

*Write **ONE WORD ONLY** for each answer.*

Listening test audio

Space Traffic Management

A Space Traffic Management system

- is a concept similar to Air Traffic Control, but for satellites rather than planes.

- would aim to set up legal and **31** .... ways of improving safety.

- does not actually exist at present.

Problems in developing effective Space Traffic Management

- Satellites are now quite **32** .... and therefore more widespread (e.g. there are constellations made up of **33** .... of satellites).

- At present, satellites are not required to transmit information to help with their **34** ....

- There are few systems for **35** .... satellites.

- Small pieces of debris may be difficult to identify.

- Operators may be unwilling to share details of satellites used for **36** .... or commercial reasons.

- It may be hard to collect details of the object's **37** .... at a given time.

- Scientists can only make a **38** .... about where the satellite will go.

Solutions

- Common standards should be agreed on for the presentation of information.

- The information should be combined in one **39** ....

- A coordinated system must be designed to create **40** .... in its users.

→ 🔊 p. 123   📄 p. 113

READING PASSAGE 1

*You should spend about 20 minutes on **Questions 1–13**, which are based on Reading Passage 1 below.*

Materials to take us beyond concrete

Concrete is everywhere, but it's bad for the planet, generating large amounts of carbon dioxide – alternatives are being developed

A Concrete is the second most used substance in the global economy, after water – and one of the world's biggest single sources of greenhouse gas emissions. The chemical process by which cement, the key ingredient of concrete, is created results in large quantities of carbon dioxide. The UN estimates that there will be 9.8 billion people living on the planet by mid-century. They will need somewhere to live. If concrete is the only answer to the construction of new cities, then carbon emissions will soar, aggravating global warming. And so scientists have started innovating with other materials, in a scramble for alternatives to a universal commodity that has underpinned our modern life for many years.

B The problem with replacing concrete is that it is so very good at what it does. Chris Cheeseman, an engineering professor at Imperial College London, says the key thing to consider is the extent to which concrete is used around the world, and is likely to continue to be used. 'Concrete is not a high-carbon product. Cement is high carbon, but concrete is not. But it is the scale on which it is used that makes it high carbon. The sheer scale of manufacture is so huge, that is the issue.'

C Not only are the ingredients of concrete relatively cheap and found in abundance in most places around the globe, the stuff itself has marvellous properties: Portland cement, the vital component of concrete, is mouldable and pourable, but quickly sets hard. Cheeseman also notes another advantage: concrete and steel have similar thermal expansion properties, so steel can be used to reinforce concrete, making it far stronger and more flexible as a building material than it could be on its own. According to Cheeseman, all these factors together make concrete hard to beat. 'Concrete is amazing stuff. Making anything with similar properties is going to be very difficult.'

D A possible alternative to concrete is wood. Making buildings from wood may seem like a rather medieval idea, but climate change is driving architects to turn to treated timber as a possible resource. Recent years have seen the emergence of tall buildings constructed almost entirely from timber. Vancouver, Vienna and Brumunddal in Norway are all home to constructed tall, wooden buildings.

E   Using wood to construct buildings, however, is not straightforward. Wood expands as it absorbs moisture from the air and is susceptible to pests, not to mention fire. But treating wood and combining it with other materials can improve its properties. Cross-laminated timber is engineered wood. An adhesive is used to stick layers of solid-sawn timber together, crosswise, to form building blocks. This material is light but has the strength of concrete and steel. Construction experts say that wooden buildings can be constructed at a greater speed than ones of concrete and steel and the process, it seems, is quieter.

F   Stora Enso is Europe's biggest supplier of cross-laminated timber, and its vice-president Markus Mannström reports that the company is seeing increasing demand globally for building in wood, with climate change concerns the key driver. Finland, with its large forests, where Stora Enso is based, has been leading the way, but the company is seeing a rise in demand for its timber products across the world, including in Asia. Of course, using timber in a building also locks away the carbon that it absorbed as it grew. But even treated wood has its limitations and only when a wider range of construction projects has been proven in practice will it be possible to see wood as a real alternative to concrete in constructing tall buildings.

G   Fly ash and slag from iron ore are possible alternatives to cement in a concrete mix. Fly ash, a byproduct of coal-burning power plants, can be incorporated into concrete mixes to make up as much as 15 to 30% of the cement, without harming the strength or durability of the resulting mix. Iron-ore slag, a byproduct of the iron-ore smelting process, can be used in a similar way. Their incorporation into concrete mixes has the potential to reduce greenhouse gas emissions.

But Anna Surgenor, of the UK's Green Building Council, notes that although these waste products can save carbon in the concrete mix, their use is not always straightforward. 'It's possible to replace the cement content in concrete with waste products to lower the overall carbon impact. But there are several calculations that need to be considered across the entire life cycle of the building – these include factoring in where these materials are being shipped from. If they are transported over long distances, using fossil fuels, the use of alternative materials might not make sense from an overall carbon reduction perspective.'

H   While these technologies are all promising ideas, they are either unproven or based on materials that are not abundant. In their overview of innovation in the concrete industry, Felix Preston and Johanna Lehne of the UK's Royal Institute of International Affairs reached the conclusion that, 'Some novel cements have been discussed for more than a decade within the research community, without breaking through. At present, these alternatives are rarely as cost-effective as conventional cement, and they face raw-material shortages and resistance from customers.'

Questions 1–4

Reading Passage 1 has eight sections, **A–H**.

Which section contains the following information?

*Write the correct letter, **A–H**, in boxes 1–4 on your answer sheet.*

1   an explanation of the industrial processes that create potential raw materials for concrete

2   a reference to the various locations where high-rise wooden buildings can be found

3   an indication of how widely available the raw materials of concrete are

4   the belief that more high-rise wooden buildings are needed before wood can be regarded as a viable construction material

Questions 5–8

Complete the summary below.

*Choose **ONE WORD ONLY** from the passage for each answer.*

Write your answers in boxes 5–8 on your answer sheet.

Making buildings with wood

Wood is a traditional building material, but current environmental concerns are encouraging **5** .... to use wood in modern construction projects. Using wood, however, has its challenges. For example, as **6** .... in the atmosphere enters wood, it increases in size. In addition, wood is prone to pests and the risk of fire is greater. However, wood can be turned into a better construction material if it is treated and combined with other materials. In one process, **7** .... of solid wood are glued together to create building blocks. These blocks are lighter than concrete and steel but equal them in strength. Experts say that wooden buildings are an improvement on those made of concrete and steel in terms of the **8** .... with which they can be constructed and how much noise is generated by the process.

Questions 9–13

Look at the following statements (Questions 9–13) and the list of people below.

*Match each statement with the correct person, **A**, **B**, **C** or **D**.*

*Write the correct letter, **A**, **B**, **C** or **D**, in boxes 9–13 on your answer sheet.*

NB *You may use any letter more than once.*

9 The environmental advantage of cement alternatives may not be as great as initially assumed.

10 It would be hard to create a construction alternative to concrete that offers so many comparable benefits.

11 Worries about the environment have led to increased interest in wood as a construction material.

12 Expense has been a factor in the negative response to the development of new cements.

13 The environmental damage caused by concrete is due to it being produced in large quantities.

List of People
A Chris Cheeseman
B Markus Mannström
C Anna Surgenor
D Felix Preston and Johanna Lehne

READING PASSAGE 2

*You should spend about 20 minutes on **Questions 14–26**, which are based on Reading Passage 2 on pages 66 and 67.*

Questions 14–20

Reading Passage 2 has seven paragraphs, **A–G**.

Choose the correct heading for each paragraph from the list of headings below.

*Write the correct number, **i–viii**, in boxes 14–20 on your answer sheet.*

List of Headings

i   A period in cold conditions before the technology is assessed

ii   Marketing issues lead to failure

iii   Good and bad aspects of steam technology are passed on

iv   A possible solution to the issues of today

v   Further improvements lead to commercial orders

vi   Positive publicity at last for this quiet, clean, fast vehicle

vii   A disappointing outcome for customers

viii   A better option than the steam car arises

---

14   Paragraph **A**

15   Paragraph **B**

16   Paragraph **C**

17   Paragraph **D**

18   Paragraph **E**

19   Paragraph **F**

20   Paragraph **G**

The steam car

The successes and failures of the Doble brothers and their steam cars

A   When primitive automobiles first began to appear in the 1800s, their engines were based on steam power. Steam had already enjoyed a long and successful career in the railways, so it was only natural that the technology evolved into a miniaturized version which was separate from the trains. But these early cars inherited steam's weaknesses along with its strengths. The boilers had to be lit by hand, and they required about twenty minutes to build up pressure before they could be driven. Furthermore, their water reservoirs only lasted for about thirty miles before needing replenishment. Despite such shortcomings, these newly designed self-propelled carriages offered quick transportation, and by the early 1900s it was not uncommon to see such machines shuttling wealthy citizens around town.

B   But the glory days of steam cars were few. A new technology called the Internal Combustion Engine soon appeared, which offered the ability to drive down the road just moments after starting up. At first, these noisy gasoline cars were unpopular because they were more complicated to operate and they had difficult hand-crank starters, which were known to break arms when the engines backfired. But in 1912 General Motors introduced the electric starter, and over the following few years steam power was gradually phased out.

C   Even as the market was declining, four brothers made one last effort to rekindle the technology. Between 1906 and 1909, while still attending high school, Abner Doble and his three brothers built their first steam car in their parents' basement. It comprised parts taken from a wrecked early steam car but reconfigured to drive an engine of their own design. Though it did not run well, the Doble brothers went on to build a second and third prototype in the following years. Though the Doble boys' third prototype, nicknamed the Model B, still lacked the convenience of an internal combustion engine, it drew the attention of automobile trade magazines due to its numerous improvements over previous steam cars. The Model B proved to be superior to gasoline automobiles in many ways. Its high-pressure steam drove the engine pistons in virtual silence, in contrast to clattering gas engines which emitted the aroma of burned hydrocarbons. Perhaps most impressively, the Model B was amazingly swift. It could accelerate from zero to sixty miles per hour in just fifteen seconds, a feat described as 'remarkable acceleration' by *Automobile* magazine in 1914.

D   The following year Abner Doble drove the Model B from Massachusetts to Detroit in order to seek investment in his automobile design, which he used to open the General Engineering Company. He and his brothers immediately began working on the Model C, which was intended to expand upon the innovations of the Model B. The brothers added features such as a key-based ignition in the cabin, eliminating the need for the operator to manually ignite the boiler. With these enhancements, the Dobles' new car company promised a steam vehicle which would provide all of the convenience of a gasoline car, but with much greater speed, much simpler driving controls, and a virtually silent powerplant. By the following April, the General Engineering Company had received 5,390 deposits for Doble Detroits, which were scheduled for delivery in early 1918.

E   Later that year Abner Doble delivered unhappy news to those eagerly awaiting the delivery of their modern new cars. Those buyers who received the handful of completed cars complained that the vehicles were sluggish and erratic, sometimes going in reverse when they should go forward. The new engine design, though innovative, was still plagued with serious glitches.

F   The brothers made one final attempt to produce a viable steam automobile. In early 1924, the Doble brothers shipped a Model E to New York City to be road-tested by the Automobile Club of America. After sitting overnight in freezing temperatures, the car was pushed out into the road and left to sit for over an hour in the frosty morning air. At the turn of the key, the boiler lit and reached its operating pressure inside of forty seconds. As they drove the test vehicle further, they found that its evenly distributed weight lent it surprisingly good handling, even though it was so heavy. As the new Doble steamer was further developed and tested, its maximum speed was pushed to over a hundred miles per hour, and it achieved about fifteen miles per gallon of kerosene with negligible emissions.

G   Sadly, the Dobles' brilliant steam car never was a financial success. Priced at around $18,000 in 1924, it was popular only among the very wealthy. Plus, it is said that no two Model Es were quite the same, because Abner Doble tinkered endlessly with the design. By the time the company folded in 1931, fewer than fifty of the amazing Model E steam cars had been produced. For his whole career, until his death in 1961, Abner Doble remained adamant that steam-powered automobiles were at least equal to gasoline cars, if not superior. Given the evidence, he may have been right. Many of the Model E Dobles which have survived are still in good working condition, some having been driven over half a million miles with only normal maintenance. Astonishingly, an unmodified Doble Model E runs clean enough to pass the emissions laws in California today, and they are pretty strict. It is true that the technology poses some difficult problems, but you cannot help but wonder how efficient a steam car might be with the benefit of modern materials and computers. Under the current pressure to improve automotive performance and reduce emissions, it is not unthinkable that the steam car may rise again.

Questions 21–23

*Choose the correct letter, **A, B, C** or **D**.*

Write the correct letter in boxes 21–23 on your answer sheet.

21 What point does the writer make about the steam car in Paragraph B?

    A   Its success was short-lived.
    B   Not enough cars were made.
    C   Car companies found them hard to sell.
    D   People found them hard to drive.

22 When building their first steam car, the Doble brothers

    A   constructed all the parts themselves.
    B   made written notes at each stage of the construction.
    C   needed several attempts to achieve a competitive model.
    D   sought the advice of experienced people in the car industry.

23 In order to produce the Model C, the Doble brothers

    A   moved production to a different city.
    B   raised financial capital.
    C   employed an additional worker.
    D   abandoned their earlier designs.

Questions 24–26

Complete the summary below.

*Choose **ONE WORD AND/OR A NUMBER** from the passage for each answer.*

Write your answers in boxes 24–26 on your answer sheet.

The Model E

The Model E was road-tested in 1924 by the Automobile Club of America. They found it easy to drive, despite its weight, and it impressed the spectators. A later version of the Model E raised its **24** ...., while keeping its emissions extremely low.

The steam car was too expensive for many people and its design was constantly being altered. Under **25** .... cars were produced before the company went out of business. However, even today, there are Model Es on the road in the US. They are straightforward to maintain, and they satisfy California's **26** .... emissions laws. Perhaps today's technology and materials would help us revive the steam car.

→ 🔾 p. 124

READING PASSAGE 3

*You should spend about 20 minutes on **Questions 27–40**, which are based on Reading Passage 3 below.*

The case for mixed-ability classes

Picture this scene. It's an English literature lesson in a UK school, and the teacher has just read an extract from Shakespeare's *Romeo and Juliet* with a class of 15-year-olds. He's given some of the students copies of *No Fear Shakespeare,* a kid-friendly translation of the original. For three students, even these literacy demands are beyond them. Another girl simply can't focus and he gives her pens and paper to draw with. The teacher can ask the *No Fear* group to identify the key characters and maybe provide a tentative plot summary. He can ask most of the class about character development, and five of them might be able to support their statements with textual evidence. Now two curious students are wondering whether Shakespeare advocates living a life of moderation or one of passionate engagement.

As a teacher myself, I'd think my lesson would be going rather well if the discussion went as described above. But wouldn't this kind of class work better if there weren't a such a huge gap between the top and the bottom? If we put all the kids who needed literacy support into one class, and all the students who want to discuss the virtue of moderation into another?

The practice of 'streaming', or 'tracking', involves separating students into classes depending on their diagnosed levels of attainment. At a macro level, it requires the establishment of academically selective schools for the brightest students, and comprehensive schools for the rest. Within schools, it means selecting students into a 'stream' of general ability, or 'sets' of subject-specific ability. The practice is intuitively appealing to almost every stakeholder.

I have heard the mixed-ability model attacked by way of analogy: a group hike. The fittest in the group take the lead and set a brisk pace, only to have to stop and wait every 20 minutes. This is frustrating, and their enthusiasm wanes. Meanwhile, the slowest ones are not only embarrassed but physically struggling to keep up. What's worse, they never get a long enough break. They honestly just want to quit. Hiking, they feel, is not for them.

Mixed-ability classes bore students, frustrate parents and burn out teachers. The brightest ones will never summit Mount Everest, and the stragglers won't enjoy the lovely stroll in the park they are perhaps more suited to. Individuals suffer at the demands of the collective, mediocrity prevails. So: is learning like hiking?

The current pedagogical paradigm is arguably that of constructivism, which emerged out of the work of psychologist Lev Vygotsky. In the 1930s, Vygotsky emphasised the importance of targeting a student's specific 'zone of proximal development' (ZPD). This is the gap between what they can achieve only with support – teachers, textbooks, worked examples, parents and so on – and what they can achieve independently. The purpose of teaching is to provide and then gradually remove this 'scaffolding' until they are autonomous. If we accept this model, it follows that streaming students with similar ZPDs would be an efficient and effective solution. And that forcing everyone on the same hike – regardless of aptitude – would be madness.

Despite all this, there is limited empirical evidence to suggest that streaming results in

70

better outcomes for students. Professor John Hattie, director of the Melbourne Education Research Institute, notes that 'tracking has minimal effects on learning outcomes'. What is more, streaming appears to significantly – and negatively – affect those students assigned to the lowest sets. These students tend to have much higher representation of low socioeconomic class. Less significant is the small benefit for those lucky clever students in the higher sets. The overall result is that the smart stay smart and the dumb get dumber, further entrenching the social divide.

In the latest update of Hattie's influential meta-analysis of factors influencing student achievement, one of the most significant factors is the teachers' estimate of achievement. Streaming students by diagnosed achievement automatically limits what the teacher feels the student is capable of. Meanwhile, in a mixed environment, teachers' estimates need to be more diverse and flexible.

While streaming might seem to help teachers effectively target a student's ZPD, it can underestimate the importance of peer-to-peer learning. A crucial aspect of constructivist theory is the role of the MKO – 'more-knowledgeable other' – in knowledge construction. While teachers are traditionally the MKOs in classrooms, the value of knowledgeable student peers must not go unrecognised either.

I find it amazing to watch students get over an idea to their peers in ways that I would never think of. They operate with different language tools and different social tools from teachers and, having just learnt it themselves, they possess similar cognitive structures to their struggling classmates. There is also something exciting about passing on skills and knowledge that you yourself have just mastered – a certain pride and zeal, a certain freshness to the interaction between 'teacher' and 'learner' that is often lost by the expert for whom the steps are obvious and the joy of discovery forgotten.

Having a variety of different abilities in a collaborative learning environment provides valuable resources for helping students meet their learning needs, not to mention improving their communication and social skills. And today, more than ever, we need the many to flourish – not suffer at the expense of a few bright stars. Once a year, I go on a hike with my class, a mixed bunch of students. It *is* challenging. The fittest students realise they need to encourage the reluctant. There are lookouts who report back, and extra items to carry for others. We make it – together.

Questions 27–30

*Choose the correct letter, **A**, **B**, **C** or **D**.*

Write the correct letter in boxes 27–30 on your answer sheet.

27 The writer describes the *Romeo and Juliet* lesson in order to demonstrate

    A   how few students are interested in literature.
    B   how a teacher handles a range of learning needs.
    C   how unsuitable Shakespeare is for most teenagers.
    D   how weaker students can disrupt their classmates' learning.

28 What does the writer say about streaming in the third paragraph?

    A   It has a very broad appeal.
    B   It favours cleverer students.
    C   It is relatively simple to implement.
    D   It works better in some schools than others.

29 What idea is suggested by the reference to Mount Everest in the fifth paragraph?

    A   students following unsuitable paths
    B   students attempting interesting tasks
    C   students not achieving their full potential
    D   students not being aware of their limitations

30 What does the word 'scaffolding' in the sixth paragraph refer to?

    A   the factors which prevent a student from learning effectively
    B   the environment where most of a student's learning takes place
    C   the assistance given to a student in their initial stages of learning
    D   the setting of appropriate learning targets for a student's aptitude

Questions 31–35

*Complete the summary using the list of phrases, **A–I**, below.*

*Write the correct letter, **A–I**, in boxes 31–35 on your answer sheet.*

Is streaming effective?

According to Professor John Hattie of the Melbourne Education Research Institute, there is very little indication that streaming leads to **31** .... He points out that, in schools which use streaming, the most significant impact is on those students placed in the **32** .... , especially where a large proportion of them have **33** .... Meanwhile, for the **34** .... , there appears to be only minimal advantage. A further issue is that teachers tend to have **35** .... of students in streamed groups.

A	wrong classes	**B**	lower expectations	**C**	average learners
D	bottom sets	**E**	brightest pupils	**F**	disadvantaged backgrounds
G	weaker students	**H**	higher achievements	**I**	positive impressions

Questions 36–40

Do the following statements agree with the views of the writer in Reading Passage 3?

In boxes 36–40 on your answer sheet, write

> **YES**   *if the statement agrees with the views of the writer*
> **NO**   *if the statement contradicts the views of the writer*
> **NOT GIVEN** *if it is impossible to say what the writer thinks about this*

36 The Vygotsky model of education supports the concept of a mixed-ability class.

37 Some teachers are uncertain about allowing students to take on MKO roles in the classroom.

38 It can be rewarding to teach knowledge which you have only recently acquired.

39 The priority should be to ensure that the highest-achieving students attain their goals.

40 Taking part in collaborative outdoor activities with teachers and classmates can improve student outcomes in the classroom.

WRITING TASK 1

You should spend about 20 minutes on this task.

> *The diagram below shows the floor plan of a public library 20 years ago and how it looks now.*
>
> *Summarise the information by selecting and reporting the main features, and make comparisons where relevant.*

Write at least 150 words.

Central Library 20 years ago

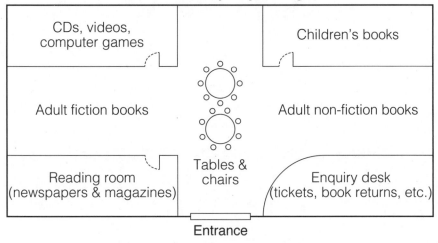

Central Library today

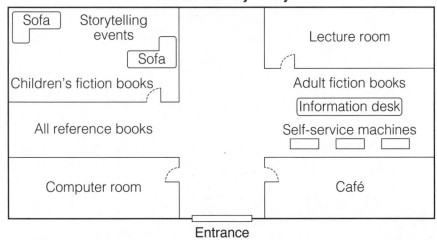

WRITING TASK 2

You should spend about 40 minutes on this task.

Write about the following topic:

> **In many countries around the world, rural people are moving to cities, so the population in the countryside is decreasing.**
>
> **Do you think this is a positive or a negative development?**

Give reasons for your answer and include any relevant examples from your own knowledge or experience.

Write at least 250 words.

SPEAKING

PART 1

The examiner asks you about yourself, your home, work or studies and other familiar topics.

EXAMPLE

Online shopping

- How often do you buy things online? [Why?]
- What was the last thing you bought online?
- Do you ever see things in shops and then buy them online? [Why/Why not?]
- Do you think the popularity of online shopping is changing your town or city centre? [Why/Why not?]

PART 2

Describe a time when you enjoyed visiting a member of your family in their home.

You should say:
    who you visited and where they lived
    why you made this visit
    what happened during this visit

and explain what you enjoyed about this visit.

You will have to talk about the topic for one to two minutes. You have one minute to think about what you are going to say. You can make some notes to help you if you wish.

PART 3

Discussion topics:

Family occasions

Example questions:
When do families celebrate together in your country?
How often do all the generations in a family come together in your country?
Why is it that some people might *not* enjoy attending family occasions?

Everyday life in families

Example questions:
Do you think it is a good thing for parents to help their children with schoolwork?
How important do you think it is for families to eat together at least once a day?
Do you believe that everyone in a family should share household tasks?

Test 4

PART 1   *Questions 1–10*

Complete the notes below.

*Write **ONE WORD AND/OR A NUMBER** for each answer.*

Listening test audio

Job details from employment agency

Role   **1** ....

Location   Fordham **2** .... Centre

                 3 .... Road, Fordham

Work involves

- dealing with enquiries
- making **4** .... and reorganising them
- maintaining the internal **5** ....
- general administration

Requirements

- **6** .... (essential)
- a calm and **7** .... manner
- good IT skills

Other information

- a **8** .... job – further opportunities may be available
- hours: 7.45 a.m. to **9** .... p.m. Monday to Friday
- **10** .... is available onsite

PART 2   *Questions 11–20*

Questions 11–14

*Choose the correct letter, **A**, **B** or **C**.*

Listening test audio

11   The museum building was originally

    A   a factory.
    B   a private home.
    C   a hall of residence.

12   The university uses part of the museum building as

    A   teaching rooms.
    B   a research library.
    C   administration offices.

13   What does the guide say about the entrance fee?

    A   Visitors decide whether or not they wish to pay.
    B   Only children and students receive a discount.
    C   The museum charges extra for special exhibitions.

14   What are visitors advised to leave in the cloakroom?

    A   cameras
    B   coats
    C   bags

Questions 15–20

What information does the speaker give about each of the following areas of the museum?

*Choose **SIX** answers from the box and write the correct letter, **A–H**, next to Questions 15–20.*

Information
A Parents must supervise their children.
B There are new things to see.
C It is closed today.
D This is only for school groups.
E There is a quiz for visitors.
F It features something created by students.
G An expert is here today.
H There is a one-way system.

Areas of museum

15 Four Seasons ....

16 Farmhouse Kitchen ....

17 A Year on the Farm ....

18 Wagon Walk ....

19 Bees are Magic ....

20 The Pond ....

 → p. 125 p. 115

PART 3   *Questions 21–30*

Listening test audio

Questions 21 and 22

*Choose **TWO** letters, **A–E**.*

Which **TWO** educational skills were shown in the video of children doing origami?

- **A**   solving problems
- **B**   following instructions
- **C**   working cooperatively
- **D**   learning through play
- **E**   developing hand–eye coordination

Questions 23–27

Which comment do the students make about each of the following children in the video?

*Choose **SIX** answers from the box and write the correct letter, **A–G**, next to Questions 23–27.*

Comments
A   demonstrated independence
B   asked for teacher support
C   developed a competitive attitude
D   seemed to find the activity calming
E   seemed pleased with the results
F   seemed confused
G   seemed to find the activity easy

Children

23   Sid   ....

24   Jack   ....

25   Naomi   ....

26   Anya   ....

27   Zara   ....

Questions 28–30

*Choose the correct letter, **A**, **B** or **C**.*

28 Before starting an origami activity in class, the students think it is important for the teacher to

    A   make models that demonstrate the different stages.
    B   check children understand the terminology involved.
    C   tell children not to worry if they find the activity difficult.

29 The students agree that some teachers might be unwilling to use origami in class because

    A   they may not think that crafts are important.
    B   they may not have the necessary skills.
    C   they may worry that it will take up too much time.

30 Why do the students decide to use origami in their maths teaching practice?

    A   to correct a particular misunderstanding
    B   to set a challenge
    C   to introduce a new concept

PART 4   *Questions 31–40*

Complete the notes below.

*Write **ONE WORD ONLY** for each answer.*

Listening test audio

Victor Hugo

His novel, *Les Misérables*

*   It has been adapted for theatre and cinema.

*   We know more about its overall **31** .... than about its author.

His early career

*   In Paris, his career was successful and he led the Romantic movement.

*   He spoke publicly about social issues, such as **32** .... and education.

*   Napoleon III disliked his views and exiled him.

His exile from France

*   Victor Hugo had to live elsewhere in **33** ....

*   He used his income from the sale of some **34** .... he had written to buy a house on Guernsey.

His house on Guernsey

*   Victor Hugo lived in this house until the end of the Empire in France.

*   The ground floor contains portraits, **35** .... and tapestries that he valued.

*   He bought cheap **36** .... made of wood and turned this into beautiful wall carvings.

*   The first floor consists of furnished areas with wallpaper and **37** .... that have a Chinese design.

*   The library still contains many of his favourite books.

*   He wrote in a room at the top of the house that had a view of the **38** ....

*   He entertained other writers as well as poor **39** .... in his house.

*   Victor Hugo's **40** .... gave ownership of the house to the city of Paris in 1927.

→ 🔍 p. 125 | 📋 p. 117

READING

READING PASSAGE 1

*You should spend about 20 minutes on **Questions 1–13**, which are based on Reading Passage 1 below.*

Green roofs

A   Rooftops covered with grass, vegetable gardens and lush foliage are now a common sight in many cities around the world. More and more private companies and city authorities are investing in green roofs, drawn to their wide-ranging benefits. Among the benefits are saving on energy costs, mitigating the risk of floods, making habitats for urban wildlife, tackling air pollution and even growing food. These increasingly radical urban designs can help cities adapt to the monumental problems they face, such as access to resources and a lack of green space due to development. But the involvement of city authorities, businesses and other institutions is crucial to ensuring their success – as is research investigating different options to suit the variety of rooftop spaces found in cities. The UK is relatively new to developing green roofs, and local governments and institutions are playing a major role in spreading the practice. London is home to much of the UK's green roof market, mainly due to forward-thinking policies such as the London Plan, which has paved the way to more than doubling the area of green roofs in the capital.

B   Ongoing research is showcasing how green roofs in cities can integrate with 'living walls': environmentally friendly walls which are partially or completely covered with greenery, including a growing medium, such as soil or water. Research also indicates that green roofs can be integrated with drainage systems on the ground, such as street trees, so that the water is managed better and the built environment is made more sustainable. There is also evidence to demonstrate the social value of green roofs. Doctors are increasingly prescribing time spent gardening outdoors for patients dealing with anxiety and depression. And research has found that access to even the most basic green spaces can provide a better quality of life for dementia sufferers and help people avoid obesity.

C   In North America, green roofs have become mainstream, with a wide array of expansive, accessible and food-producing roofs installed in buildings. Again, city leaders and authorities have helped push the movement forward – only recently, San Francisco, USA, created a policy requiring new buildings to have green roofs. Toronto, Canada, has policies dating from the 1990s, encouraging the development of urban farms on rooftops. These countries also benefit from having newer buildings than in many parts of the world, which makes it easier to install green roofs. Being able to keep enough water at roof height and distribute it right across the rooftop is crucial to maintaining the plants on any green roof – especially on 'edible roofs' where fruit and vegetables are farmed. And it's much easier to do this in newer buildings, which can typically hold greater weight, than to retro-fit old ones. Having a stronger roof also makes it easier to grow a greater variety of plants, since the soil can be deeper.

D   For green roofs to become the norm for new developments, there needs to be support from public authorities and private investors. Those responsible for maintaining buildings may have to acquire new skills, such as landscaping, and in some cases, volunteers may be needed to help out. Other considerations include installing drainage paths, meeting health and safety requirements and perhaps allowing access for the public, as well as planning restrictions and disruption from regular activities in and around the buildings during installation. To convince investors and developers that installing green roofs is worthwhile, economic arguments are still the most important. The term 'natural capital' has been developed to explain the economic value of nature; for example, measuring the money saved by installing natural solutions to protect against flood damage, adapt to climate change or help people lead healthier and happier lives.

E   As the expertise about green roofs grows, official standards have been developed to ensure that they are designed, constructed and maintained properly, and function well. Improvements in the science and technology underpinning green roof development have also led to new variations in the concept. For example, 'blue roofs' enable buildings to hold water over longer periods of time, rather than draining it away quickly – crucial in times of heavier rainfall. There are also combinations of green roofs with solar panels, and 'brown roofs' which are wilder in nature and maximise biodiversity. If the trend continues, it could create new jobs and a more vibrant and sustainable local food economy – alongside many other benefits. There are still barriers to overcome, but the evidence so far indicates that green roofs have the potential to transform cities and help them function sustainably long into the future. The success stories need to be studied and replicated elsewhere, to make green, blue, brown and food-producing roofs the norm in cities around the world.

Questions 1–5

Reading Passage 1 has five paragraphs, **A–E**.

Which paragraph contains the following information?

*Write the correct letter, **A–E**, in boxes 1–5 on your answer sheet.*

NB *You may use any letter more than once.*

1   mention of several challenges to be overcome before a green roof can be installed

2   reference to a city where green roofs have been promoted for many years

3   a belief that existing green roofs should be used as a model for new ones

4   examples of how green roofs can work in combination with other green urban initiatives

5   the need to make a persuasive argument for the financial benefits of green roofs

Questions 6–9

Complete the summary below.

*Choose **ONE WORD ONLY** from the passage for each answer.*

Write your answers in boxes 6–9 on your answer sheet.

Advantages of green roofs

City rooftops covered with greenery have many advantages. These include lessening the likelihood that floods will occur, reducing how much money is spent on **6** .... and creating environments that are suitable for wildlife. In many cases, they can also be used for producing **7** ....

There are also social benefits of green roofs. For example, the medical profession recommends **8** .... as an activity to help people cope with mental health issues. Studies have also shown that the availability of green spaces can prevent physical problems such as **9** ....

Questions 10 and 11

*Choose **TWO** letters, **A–E**.*

Write the correct letters in boxes 10 and 11 on your answer sheet.

Which **TWO** advantages of using newer buildings for green roofs are mentioned in Paragraph C of the passage?

    A   a longer growing season for edible produce
    B   more economical use of water
    C   greater water-storage capacity
    D   ability to cultivate more plant types
    E   a large surface area for growing plants

Questions 12 and 13

*Choose **TWO** letters, **A–E**.*

Write the correct letters in boxes 12 and 13 on your answer sheet.

Which **TWO** aims of new variations on the concept of green roofs are mentioned in Paragraph E of the passage?

    A   to provide habitats for a wide range of species
    B   to grow plants successfully even in the wettest climates
    C   to regulate the temperature of the immediate environment
    D   to generate power from a sustainable source
    E   to collect water to supply other buildings

→ ◐ p. 126

READING PASSAGE 2

*You should spend about 20 minutes on **Questions 14–26**, which are based on Reading Passage 2 below.*

The growth mindset

Over the past century, a powerful idea has taken root in the educational landscape. The concept of intelligence as something innate has been supplanted by the idea that intelligence is not fixed, and that, with the right training, we can be the authors of our own cognitive capabilities. Psychologist Alfred Binet, the developer of the first intelligence tests, was one of many 19th-century scientists who held that earlier view and sought to quantify cognitive ability. Then, in the early 20th century, progressive thinkers revolted against the notion that inherent ability is destiny. Instead, educators such as John Dewey argued that every child's intelligence could be developed, given the right environment.

'Growth mindset theory' is a relatively new – and extremely popular – version of this idea. In many schools today you will see hallways covered in motivational posters and hear speeches on the mindset of great sporting heroes who simply *believed* their way to the top. A major focus of the growth mindset in schools is coaxing students away from seeing failure as an indication of their ability, and towards seeing it as a chance to improve that ability. As educationalist Jeff Howard noted several decades ago: 'Smart is not something that you just are, smart is something that you can get.'

The idea of the growth mindset is based on the work of psychologist Carol Dweck in California in the 1990s. In one key experiment, Dweck divided a group of 10- to 12-year-olds into two groups. All were told that they had achieved a high score on a test but the first group were praised for their intelligence in achieving this, while the others were praised for their effort. The second group – those who had been instilled with a 'growth mindset' – were subsequently far more likely to put effort into future tasks. Meanwhile, the former took on only those tasks that would not risk their sense of worth. This group had inferred that success or failure is due to innate ability, and this 'fixed mindset' had led them to fear of failure and lack of effort. Praising ability actually made the students perform worse, while praising effort emphasised that change was possible.

One of the greatest impediments to successfully implementing a growth mindset, however, is the education system itself: in many parts of the world, the school climate is obsessed with performance in the form of constant testing, analysing and ranking of students – a key characteristic of the fixed mindset. Nor is it unusual for schools to create a certain cognitive dissonance, when they applaud the benefits of a growth mindset but then hand out fixed target grades in lessons based on performance.

Aside from the implementation problem, the original growth mindset research has also received harsh criticism. The statistician Andrew Gelman claims that 'their research designs have enough degrees of freedom that they could take their data to support just about any theory at all'. Professor of Psychology Timothy Bates, who has been trying to replicate Dweck's work, is finding that the results are repeatedly null. He notes that: 'People with a growth mindset don't cope any better with failure … Kids with the growth mindset aren't getting better grades, either before or after our intervention study.'

Much of this criticism is not lost on Dweck, and she deserves great credit for responding to it and adapting her work accordingly. In fact, she argues that her work has been misunderstood and misapplied in a range of ways. She has also expressed concerns that her theories are being misappropriated in schools by being conflated with the self-esteem movement: 'For me the growth mindset is a tool for learning and improvement. It's not just a vehicle for making children feel good.'

But there is another factor at work here. The failure to translate the growth mindset into the classroom might reflect a misunderstanding of the nature of teaching and learning itself. Growth mindset supporters David Yeager and Gregory Walton claim that interventions should be delivered in a subtle way to maximise their effectiveness. They say that if adolescents perceive a teacher's intervention as conveying that they are in need of help, this could undo its intended effects.

A lot of what drives students is their innate beliefs and how they perceive themselves. There is a strong correlation between self-perception and achievement, but there is evidence to suggest that the actual effect of achievement on self-perception is stronger than the other way round. To stand up in a classroom and successfully deliver a good speech is a genuine achievement, and that is likely to be more powerfully motivating than vague notions of 'motivation' itself.

Recent evidence would suggest that growth mindset interventions are not the elixir of student learning that its proponents claim it to be. The growth mindset appears to be a viable construct in the lab, which, when administered in the classroom via targeted interventions, doesn't seem to work. It is hard to dispute that having faith in the capacity to change is a good attribute for students. Paradoxically, however, that aspiration is not well served by direct interventions that try to instil it.

Motivational posters and talks are often a waste of time, and might well give students a deluded notion of what success actually means. Teaching concrete skills such as how to write an effective introduction to an essay then praising students' effort in getting there is probably a far better way of improving confidence than telling them how unique they are, or indeed how capable they are of changing their own brains. Perhaps growth mindset works best as a philosophy and not an intervention.

Questions 14–16

*Choose the correct letter, **A**, **B**, **C** or **D**.*

Write the correct letter in boxes 14–16 on your answer sheet.

14   What can we learn from the first paragraph?

  A   where the notion of innate intelligence first began
  B   when ideas about the nature of intelligence began to shift
  C   how scientists have responded to changing views of intelligence
  D   why thinkers turned away from the idea of intelligence being fixed

15   The second paragraph describes how schools encourage students to

  A   identify their personal ambitions.
  B   help each other to realise their goals.
  C   have confidence in their potential to succeed.
  D   concentrate on where their particular strengths lie.

16   In the third paragraph, the writer suggests that students with a fixed mindset

  A   tend to be less competitive.
  B   generally have a low sense of self-esteem.
  C   will only work hard if they are given constant encouragement.
  D   are afraid to push themselves beyond what they see as their limitations.

Questions 17–22

Look at the following statements (Questions 17–22) and the list of people below.

*Match each statement with the correct person or people, **A–E**.*

*Write the correct letter, **A–E**, in boxes 17–22 on your answer sheet.*

NB *You may use any letter more than once.*

17 The methodology behind the growth mindset studies was not strict enough.

18 The idea of the growth mindset has been incorrectly interpreted.

19 Intellectual ability is an unchangeable feature of each individual.

20 The growth mindset should be promoted without students being aware of it.

21 The growth mindset is not simply about boosting students' morale.

22 Research shows that the growth mindset has no effect on academic achievement.

List of People
A   Alfred Binet
B   Carol Dweck
C   Andrew Gelman
D   Timothy Bates
E   David Yeager and Gregory Walton

Questions 23–26

Do the following statements agree with the views of the writer in Reading Passage 2?

In boxes 23–26 on your answer sheet, write

>   **YES**   *if the statement agrees with the views of the writer*
>   **NO**   *if the statement contradicts the views of the writer*
>   **NOT GIVEN** *if it is impossible to say what the writer thinks about this*

23 Dweck has handled criticisms of her work in an admirable way.

24 Students' self-perception is a more effective driver of self-confidence than actual achievement is.

25 Recent evidence about growth mindset interventions has attracted unfair coverage in the media.

26 Deliberate attempts to encourage students to strive for high achievement may have a negative effect.

→ ◎ p. 126

READING PASSAGE 3

*You should spend about 20 minutes on **Questions 27–40**, which are based on Reading Passage 3 below.*

Alfred Wegener: science, exploration and the theory of continental drift

by Mott T Greene

Introduction

This is a book about the life and scientific work of Alfred Wegener, whose reputation today rests with his theory of continental displacements, better known as 'continental drift'. Wegener proposed this theory in 1912 and developed it extensively for nearly 20 years. His book on the subject, *The Origin of Continents and Oceans*, went through four editions and was the focus of an international controversy in his lifetime and for some years after his death.

Wegener's basic idea was that many mysteries about the Earth's history could be solved if one supposed that the continents moved laterally, rather than supposing that they remained fixed in place. Wegener showed in great detail how such continental movements were plausible and how they worked, using evidence from a large number of sciences including geology, geophysics, paleontology, and climatology. Wegener's idea – that the continents move – is at the heart of the theory that guides Earth sciences today: namely plate tectonics. Plate tectonics is in many respects quite different from Wegener's proposal, in the same way that modern evolutionary theory is very different from the ideas Charles Darwin proposed in the 1850s about biological evolution. Yet plate tectonics is a descendant of Alfred Wegener's theory of continental drift, in quite the same way that modern evolutionary theory is a descendant of Darwin's theory of natural selection.

When I started writing about Wegener's life and work, one of the most intriguing things about him for me was that, although he came up with a theory on continental drift, he was not a geologist. He trained as an astronomer and pursued a career in atmospheric physics. When he proposed the theory of continental displacements in 1912, he was a lecturer in physics and astronomy at the University of Marburg, in southern Germany. However, he was not an 'unknown'. In 1906 he had set a world record (with his brother Kurt) for time aloft in a hot-air balloon: 52 hours. Between 1906 and 1908 he had taken part in a highly publicized and extremely dangerous expedition to the coast of northeast Greenland. He had also made a name for himself amongst a small circle of meteorologists and atmospheric physicists in Germany as the author of a textbook, *Thermodynamics of the Atmosphere* (1911), and of a number of interesting scientific papers.

As important as Wegener's work on continental drift has turned out to be, it was largely a sideline to his interest in atmospheric physics, geophysics, and paleoclimatology[*], and thus I have been at great pains to put Wegener's work on continental drift in the larger context of his other scientific work, and in the even larger context of atmospheric sciences in his lifetime. This is a 'continental drift book' only to the extent that Wegener was interested in that topic and later became famous for it. My treatment of his other scientific work is no less detailed, though I certainly have devoted more attention to the reception of his ideas on continental displacement, as they were much more controversial than his other work.

Readers interested in the specific detail of Wegener's career will see that he often stopped pursuing a given line of investigation (sometimes for years on end), only to pick it up later. I have tried to provide guideposts to his rapidly shifting interests by characterizing different phases of his life as careers in different sciences, which is reflected in the titles of the chapters. Thus, the index should be a sufficient guide for those interested in a particular aspect of Wegener's life but perhaps not all of it. My own feeling, however, is that the parts do not make as much sense on their own as do all of his activities taken together. In this respect I urge readers to try to experience Wegener's life as he lived it, with all the interruptions, changes of mind, and renewed efforts this entailed.

Wegener left behind a few published works but, as was standard practice, these reported the results of his work – not the journey he took to reach that point. Only a few hundred of the many thousands of letters he wrote and received in his lifetime have survived and he didn't keep notebooks or diaries that recorded his life and activities. He was not active (with a few exceptions) in scientific societies, and did not seek to find influence or advance his ideas through professional contacts and politics, spending most of his time at home in his study reading and writing, or in the field collecting observations.

Some famous scientists, such as Newton, Darwin, and Einstein, left mountains of written material behind, hundreds of notebooks and letters numbering in the tens of thousands. Others, like Michael Faraday, left extensive journals of their thoughts and speculations, parallel to their scientific notebooks. The more such material a scientist leaves behind, the better chance a biographer has of forming an accurate picture of how a scientist's ideas took shape and evolved.

I am firmly of the opinion that most of us, Wegener included, are not in any real sense the authors of our own lives. We plan, think, and act, often with apparent freedom, but most of the time our lives 'happen to us', and we only retrospectively turn this happenstance into a coherent narrative of fulfilled intentions. This book, therefore, is a story both of the life and scientific work that Alfred Wegener planned and intended and of the life and scientific work that actually 'happened to him'. These are, as I think you will soon see, not always the same thing.

---

[*] Paleoclimatology – The study of past climates

Questions 27–30

Do the following statements agree with the claims of the writer in Reading Passage 3?

In boxes 27–30 on your answer sheet, write

> **YES**　　　　if the statement agrees with the claims of the writer
> **NO**　　　　 if the statement contradicts the claims of the writer
> **NOT GIVEN**　if it is impossible to say what the writer thinks about this

27 Wegener's ideas about continental drift were widely disputed while he was alive.

28 The idea that the continents remained fixed in place was defended in a number of respected scientific publications.

29 Wegener relied on a limited range of scientific fields to support his theory of continental drift.

30 The similarities between Wegener's theory of continental drift and modern-day plate tectonics are enormous.

Questions 31–36

Complete the summary using the list of phrases, *A–J*, below.

Write the correct letter, *A–J*, in boxes 31–36 on your answer sheet.

Wegener's life and work

One of the remarkable things about Wegener from a **31** .... is that although he proposed a theory of continental drift, he was not a geologist. His **32** .... were limited to atmospheric physics. However, at the time he proposed his theory of continental drift in 1912, he was already a person of **33** .... Six years previously, there had been his **34** .... of 52 hours in a hot-air balloon, followed by his well-publicised but **35** .... of Greenland's coast. With the publication of his textbook on thermodynamics, he had also come to the attention of a **36** .... of German scientists.

A modest fame	**B** vast range	**C** record-breaking achievement	
D research methods	**E** select group	**F** professional interests	
G scientific debate	**H** hazardous exploration	**I** biographer's perspective	
J narrow investigation			

Questions 37–40

*Choose the correct letter, **A**, **B**, **C** or **D**.*

Write the correct letter in boxes 37–40 on your answer sheet.

37   What is Mott T Greene doing in the fifth paragraph?

    A   describing what motivated him to write the book
    B   explaining why it is desirable to read the whole book
    C   suggesting why Wegener pursued so many different careers
    D   indicating what aspects of Wegener's life interested him most

38   What is said about Wegener in the sixth paragraph?

    A   He was not a particularly ambitious person.
    B   He kept a record of all his scientific observations.
    C   He did not adopt many of the scientific practices of the time.
    D   He enjoyed discussing new discoveries with other scientists.

39   What does Greene say about some other famous scientists?

    A   Their published works had a greater impact than Wegener's did.
    B   They had fewer doubts about their scientific ideas than Wegener did.
    C   Their scientific ideas were more controversial than Wegener's.
    D   They are easier subjects to write about than Wegener.

40   What is Greene's main point in the final paragraph?

    A   It is not enough in life to have good intentions.
    B   People need to plan carefully if they want to succeed.
    C   People have little control over many aspects of their lives.
    D   It is important that people ensure they have the freedom to act.

→ 🔖 p. 126

WRITING

WRITING TASK 1

You should spend about 20 minutes on this task.

> *The graph below shows the average monthly change in the prices of three metals during 2014.*
>
> *Summarise the information by selecting and reporting the main features, and make comparisons where relevant.*

Write at least 150 words.

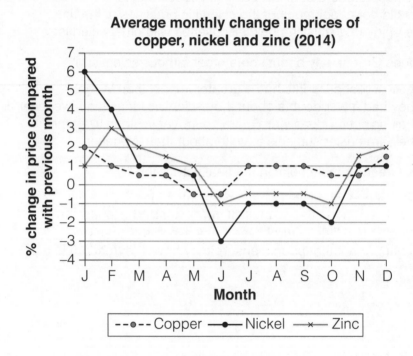

WRITING TASK 2

You should spend about 40 minutes on this task.

Write about the following topic:

> *In many countries, people are now living longer than ever before. Some people say an ageing population creates problems for governments. Other people think there are benefits if society has more elderly people.*
>
> *To what extent do the advantages of having an ageing population outweigh the disadvantages?*

Give reasons for your answer and include any relevant examples from your own knowledge or experience.

Write at least 250 words.

SPEAKING

PART 1

The examiner asks you about yourself, your home, work or studies and other familiar topics.

EXAMPLE

Sleep

- How many hours do you usually sleep at night?
- Do you sometimes sleep during the day? [Why/Why not?]
- What do you do if you can't get to sleep at night? [Why?]
- Do you ever remember the dreams you've had while you were asleep?

PART 2

Describe a time when you met someone who you became good friends with.

You should say:
  who you met
  when and where you met this person
  what you thought about this person when you first met

and explain why you think you became good friends with this person.

You will have to talk about the topic for one to two minutes. You have one minute to think about what you are going to say. You can make some notes to help you if you wish.

PART 3

Discussion topics:

Friends at school

Example questions:
How important is it for children to have lots of friends at school?
Do you think it is wrong for parents to influence which friends their children have?
Why do you think children often choose different friends as they get older?

Making new friends

Example questions:
If a person is moving to a new town, what is a good way for them to make friends?
Can you think of any disadvantages of making new friends online?
Would you say it is harder for people to make new friends as they get older?

Audioscripts

PART 1

MAN:	Excuse me. Would you mind if I asked you some questions? We're doing a survey on transport.
SADIE:	Yes, that's OK.
MAN:	First of all, can I take your name?
SADIE:	Yes. It's Sadie Jones.
MAN:	Thanks very much. And could I have your date of birth – just the year will do, actually. Is that all right?
SADIE:	Yes, that's fine. It's 1991.
MAN:	So next your postcode, please.
SADIE:	It's <u>DW30 7YZ</u>.
MAN:	Great. Thanks. Is that in Wells?
SADIE:	No it's actually in Harborne – Wells isn't far from there, though.
MAN:	I really like that area. My grandmother lived there when I was a kid.
SADIE:	Yes, it is nice.
MAN:	Right, so now I want to ask you some questions about how you travelled here today. Did you use public transport?
SADIE:	Yes. I came by bus.
MAN:	OK. And that was today. It's the <u>24th of April</u>, isn't it?
SADIE:	Isn't it the 25th? No, actually, you're right.
MAN:	Ha ha. And what was the reason for your trip today? I can see you've got some shopping with you.
SADIE:	Yes. I did some shopping but the main reason I came here was to go to the <u>dentist</u>.
MAN:	That's not much fun. Hope it was nothing serious.
SADIE:	No, it was just a check-up. It's fine.
MAN:	Good. Do you normally travel by bus into the city centre?
SADIE:	Yes. I stopped driving in ages ago because <u>parking</u> was so difficult to find and it costs so much.
MAN:	I see.
SADIE:	The bus is much more convenient too. It only takes about 30 minutes.
MAN:	That's good. So where did you start your journey?
SADIE:	At the bus stop on <u>Claxby</u> Street.
MAN:	Is that C-L-A–X-B-Y?
SADIE:	That's right.

Q1

Q2

Q3

Q4

Q5

MAN:	And how satisfied with the service are you? Do you have any complaints?
SADIE:	Well, as I said, it's very convenient and quick when it's on time, but this morning it was <u>late</u>. Only about 10 minutes, but still.
MAN:	Yes, I understand that's annoying. And what about the timetable? Do you have any comments about that?
SADIE:	Mmm. I suppose I mainly use the bus during the day, but any time I've been in town in the <u>evening</u> – for dinner or at the cinema – I've noticed you have to wait a long time for a bus – there aren't that many.

Q6

Q7

MAN:	OK, thanks. So now I'd like to ask you about your car use.	
SADIE:	Well, I have got a car but I don't use it that often. Mainly just to go to the <u>supermarket</u>. But that's about it really. My husband uses it at the weekends to go to the golf club.	Q8
MAN:	And what about a bicycle?	
SADIE:	I don't actually have one at the moment.	
MAN:	What about the city bikes you can rent? Do you ever use those?	
SADIE:	No – I'm not keen on cycling there because of all the <u>pollution</u>. But I would like to get a bike – it would be good to use it to get to work.	Q9
MAN:	So why haven't you got one now?	
SADIE:	Well, I live in a flat – on the second floor and it doesn't have any <u>storage</u> – so we'd have to leave it in the hall outside the flat.	Q10
MAN:	I see. OK. Well, I think that's all ...	

PART 2

Good evening, everyone. Let me start by welcoming you all to this talk and thanking you for taking the time to consider joining ACE voluntary organisation. ACE offers support to people and services in the local area and we're now looking for more volunteers to help us do this.

By the way, I hope you're all comfortable – <u>we have brought in extra seats so that no one has to stand, but it does mean that the people at the back of the room may be a bit squashed.</u> We'll only be here for about half an hour so, hopefully, that's OK.   Q11

One of the first questions we're often asked is how old you need to be to volunteer. Well, <u>you can be as young as 16 or you can be 60 or over</u>; it all depends on what type of voluntary work you want to do. <u>Other considerations, such as reliability, are crucial</u> in voluntary work and age isn't related to these, in our experience.   Q12

Another question we get asked relates to training. Well, there's plenty of that and it's all face-to-face. What's more, <u>training doesn't end when you start working for us – it takes place before, during and after periods of work</u>. Often, it's run by other experienced volunteers as managers tend to prefer to get on with other things.   Q13

Now, I would ask *you* to consider a couple of important issues before you decide to apply for voluntary work. We don't worry about why you want to be a volunteer – people have many different reasons that range from getting work experience to just doing something they've always wanted to do. But <u>it is critical that you have enough hours in the day</u> for whatever role we agree is suitable for you – if being a volunteer becomes stressful then it's best not to do it at all. You may think that your income is important, but we don't ask about that. It's up to you to decide if you can work without earning money. <u>What we value is dedication</u>. Some of our most loyal volunteers earn very little themselves but still give their full energy to the work they do with us.   Q14/15   Q14/15

OK, so let's take a look at some of the work areas that we need volunteers for and the sort of things that would help you in those.

You may wish simply to help us raise money. <u>If you have the creativity to come up with an imaginative or novel way of fundraising, we'd be delighted</u>, as standing in the local streets or shops with a collection box can be rather boring!   Q16

One outdoor activity that we need volunteers for is <u>litter collection and for this it's useful if you can walk for long periods, sometimes uphill</u>. Some of our regular collectors are quite elderly, but very active and keen to protect the environment.   Q17

If you enjoy working with children, we have three vacancies for what are called 'playmates'. These volunteers help children learn about staying healthy through a range of out-of-school activities. You don't need to have children yourself, but it's good if you know something about nutrition and can give clear instructions.   *Q18*

If that doesn't appeal to you, maybe you would be interested in helping out at our story club for disabled children, especially if you have done some acting. We put on three performances a year based on books they have read and we're always looking for support with the theatrical side of this.   *Q19*

The last area I'll mention today is first aid. Volunteers who join this group can end up teaching others in vulnerable groups who may be at risk of injury. Initially, though, your priority will be to take in a lot of information and not forget any important steps or details.   *Q20*

Right, so does anyone have any questions …

PART 3

HUGO:	Hi Chantal. What did you think of the talk, then?	
CHANTAL:	Hi Hugo. I thought it was good once I'd moved seats.	
HUGO:	Oh – were the people beside you chatting or something?	
CHANTAL:	It wasn't that. I went early so that I'd get a seat and not have to stand, but then this guy sat right in front of me and he was so tall!	*Q21*
HUGO:	It's hard to see through people's heads, isn't it?	
CHANTAL:	Impossible! Anyway, to answer your question, I thought it was really interesting, especially what the speaker said about the job market.	
HUGO:	Me too. I mean we know we're going into a really competitive field so it's obvious that we may struggle to get work.	
CHANTAL:	That's right – and we know we can't all have that 'dream job'.	
HUGO:	Yeah, but it looks like there's a whole range of … areas of work that we hadn't even thought of – like fashion journalism, for instance.	*Q22*
CHANTAL:	Yeah – I wasn't expecting so many career options.	
HUGO:	Mmm. Overall, she had quite a strong message, didn't she?	
CHANTAL:	She did. She kept saying things like 'I know you all think this, but …' and then she'd tell us how it really is.	
HUGO:	Perhaps she thinks students are a bit narrow-minded about the industry.	
CHANTAL:	It was a bit harsh, though! We know it's a tough industry.	*Q23*
HUGO:	Yeah – and we're only first years, after all. We've got a lot to learn.	
CHANTAL:	Exactly. Do you think our secondary-school education should have been more career-focused?	
HUGO:	Well, we had numerous talks on careers, which was good, but none of them were very inspiring. They could have asked more people like today's speaker to talk to us.	*Q24*
CHANTAL:	I agree. We were told about lots of different careers – just when we needed to be, but not by the experts who really know stuff.	
HUGO:	So did today's talk influence your thoughts on what career you'd like to take up in the future?	
CHANTAL:	Well, I promised myself that I'd go through this course and keep an open mind till the end.	*Q25*
HUGO:	But I think it's better to pick an area of the industry now and then aim to get better and better at it.	

CHANTAL:	<u>Well, I think we'll just have to differ on that issue!</u>
HUGO:	One thing's for certain, though. From what she said, we'll be unpaid assistants in the industry for quite a long time.
CHANTAL:	Mmm.
HUGO:	<u>I'm prepared for that, aren't you</u>?
CHANTAL:	Actually, I'm not going to accept that view.
HUGO:	Really? But she *knows* it's the case – and everyone else says the same.
CHANTAL:	That doesn't mean it has to be true for me.
HUGO:	OK. Well – I hope you're right!

(Q26 appears to the right of the "I'm prepared for that, aren't you?" line)

Q26

CHANTAL:	I thought the speaker's account of her first job was fascinating.
HUGO:	Yeah – she admitted she was lucky to get work being a personal dresser for a musician. She didn't even apply for the job and there she was getting paid to choose all his clothes.
CHANTAL:	It must have felt amazing – though she said all she was looking for back then was experience, not financial reward.
HUGO:	Mmm. And then he was so mean, <u>telling her she was more interested in her own appearance than his</u>!
CHANTAL:	But – <u>she did realise he was right about that</u>, which really made me think. I'm always considering my own clothes but now I can see you should be focusing on your client!
HUGO:	She obviously regretted losing the job.
CHANTAL:	Well, as she said, <u>she should have hidden her negative feelings about him, but she didn't</u>.
HUGO:	It was really brave the way she picked herself up and took that job in retail. Fancy working in a shop after that!
CHANTAL:	Yeah – well, she recommended we all do it at some point. I guess as a designer you'd get to find out some useful information, like how big or small the average shopper is.
HUGO:	I think that's an issue for manufacturers, not designers. However, <u>it *would* be useful to know if there's a gap in the market – you know, an item that no one's stocking but that consumers are looking for</u>.
CHANTAL:	Yeah, people don't give up searching. They also take things back to the store if they aren't right.
HUGO:	Yeah. Imagine you worked in an expensive shop and <u>you found out the garments sold there were being returned because they … fell apart in the wash</u>!
CHANTAL:	<u>Yeah, it would be good to know that kind of thing</u>.
HUGO:	Yeah.

Q27/28

Q27/28

Q29/30

Q29/30

PART 4

For my presentation today I want to tell you about how groups of elephants have been moved and settled in new reserves. This is known as translocation and has been carried out in Malawi in Africa in recent years. The reason this is being done is because of overpopulation of elephants in some areas.

Overpopulation is a good problem to have and not one we tend to hear about very often. In Malawi's Majete National Park the elephant population had been wiped out by poachers, who killed the elephants for their ivory. But in 2003, the park was restocked and effective law enforcement was introduced. Since then, not a single elephant has been poached. In this safe environment, the elephant population boomed. Breeding went so well that there were more elephants than the park could support.

This led to a number of problems. Firstly, there was more competition for food, which meant that some elephants were suffering from hunger. As there was a limit to the amount of food in the national park, some elephants began looking further afield. <u>Elephants were routinely knocking down fences around the park</u>, which then had to be repaired at a significant cost.

Q31

To solve this problem, the decision was made to move dozens of elephants from Majete National Park to Nkhotakota Wildlife Park, where there were no elephants. But, obviously, attempting to move significant numbers of elephants to a new home 300 kilometres away is quite a challenge.

So how did this translocation process work in practice?

Elephants were moved in <u>groups of between eight and twenty, all belonging to one family</u>. Because relationships are very important to elephants, they all had to be moved at the same time. <u>A team of vets and park rangers flew over the park in helicopters and targeted a group, which were rounded up and directed to a designated open plain.</u>

Q32

Q33

The vets then used darts to immobilise the elephants – this was a tricky manoeuvre, as they not only had to select the right dose of tranquiliser for different-sized elephants but they had to dart the elephants as they were running around. <u>This also had to be done as quickly as possible so as to minimise the stress caused</u>. As soon as the elephants began to flop onto the ground, the team moved in to take care of them.

Q34

<u>To avoid the risk of suffocation, the team had to make sure none of the elephants were lying on their chests because their lungs could be crushed in this position. So all the elephants had to be placed on their sides.</u> One person stayed with each elephant while they waited for the vets to do checks. <u>It was very important to keep an eye on their breathing – if there were fewer than six breaths per minute, the elephant would need urgent medical attention.</u> Collars were fitted to the matriarch in each group so their movements could be tracked in their new home. <u>Measurements were taken of each elephant's tusks – elephants with large tusks would be at greater risk from poachers – and also of their feet</u>. The elephants were then taken to a recovery area before being loaded onto trucks and transported to their new home.

Q35

Q36

Q37

The elephants translocated to Nkhotakota settled in very well and the project has generally been accepted to have been a huge success – and not just for the elephants. <u>Employment prospects have improved enormously, contributing to rising living standards for the whole community</u>. Poaching is no longer an issue, as former poachers are able to find more reliable sources of income. In fact, <u>many of them volunteered to give up their weapons, as they were no longer of any use to them</u>.

Q38

Q39

More than two dozen elephants have been born at Nkhotakota since relocation. With an area of more than 1,800 square kilometres, there's plenty of space for the elephant population to continue to grow. Their presence is also helping to rebalance Nkhotakota's damaged ecosystem and providing a sustainable conservation model, which could be replicated in other parks. <u>All this has been a big draw for tourism, which contributes five times more than the illegal wildlife trade to GDP, and this is mainly because of the elephants</u>. There's also been a dramatic rise in interest …

Q40

TEST 2

PART 1

WOMAN:	So, I understand you're interested in restaurant work?
MAN:	Yes. I've got a bit of experience and I can provide references.
WOMAN:	That's good. I can check all that later. Now, Milo's Restaurants have some vacancies at the moment. They're a really good company to work for. Lots of benefits.
MAN:	Oh right.
WOMAN:	Yes. They've got a very good reputation for looking after staff. For example, <u>all employees get training</u> – even temporary staff.
MAN:	Oh really? That's quite unusual, isn't it?
WOMAN:	Certainly is.
MAN:	And do staff get free uniforms too?
WOMAN:	Um … you just need to wear a white T-shirt and black trousers, it says here. So I guess not … But another benefit of working for a big company like this is that <u>you can get a discount at any of their restaurants</u>.
MAN:	Even at weekends?
WOMAN:	No, but you'll be working then anyway.
MAN:	Oh yes. I suppose so. Most of their restaurants are in the city centre, aren't they? So, easy to get to by bus?
WOMAN:	Yes. That's right. But if you have to do a late shift and finish work <u>after midnight, the company will pay for you to get a taxi home</u>.
MAN:	I probably won't need one. I think I'd use my bike.
WOMAN:	OK. Now, they do have some quite specific requirements for the kind of person they're looking for. Milo's is a young, dynamic company and they're really keen on creating a strong team. It's really important that you can fit in and get on well with everyone.
MAN:	Yeah. I've got no problem with that. It sounds good, actually. The last place I worked for was quite demanding too. We had to make sure we gave <u>a really high level of service</u>.
WOMAN:	That's good to hear because <u>that will be equally important at Milo's</u>. I know they want people who have an eye for detail.
MAN:	That's fine. I'm very used to working in that kind of environment.
WOMAN:	Perfect. So the only other thing that's required is good communication skills, so <u>you'll need to have a certificate in English</u>.
MAN:	Sure.

Q1
Q2
Q3
Q4
Q5

WOMAN:	OK. Let's have a look at the current job vacancies at Milo's. The first one is in <u>Wivenhoe Street</u>.
MAN:	Sorry, where?
WOMAN:	Wivenhoe. W-I-V-E-N-H-O-E. It's quite central, just off Cork Street.
MAN:	Oh right.
WOMAN:	They're looking for a breakfast supervisor.
MAN:	That would be OK.
WOMAN:	So you're probably familiar with the kind of responsibilities involved. Obviously checking that all the portions are correct, etc., and then things like <u>checking all the procedures for cleaning the equipment are being followed</u>.

Q6
Q7

MAN: OK. And what about the salary? In my last job I was getting £9.50 per hour. I was hoping to get a bit more than that.

WOMAN: Well, to begin with, you'd be getting £9.75 but that goes up to £11.25 after three months. Q8

MAN: That's not too bad. And I suppose it's a very early start?

WOMAN: Mmm. That's the only unattractive thing about this job. But then you have the afternoons and evenings free. So the restaurant starts serving breakfast from 7 a.m. And you'd have to be there at 5.30 to set everything up. But you'd be finished at 12.30.

MAN: Mmm. Well, as you say, there are advantages to that.

WOMAN: Now, you might also be interested in the job at the City Road branch. That's for a junior chef, so again a position of responsibility.

MAN: I might prefer that, actually.

WOMAN: Right, well obviously this role would involve supporting the sous chef and other senior staff. And you'd be responsible for making sure there's enough stock each week – and sorting out all the deliveries. Q9

MAN: I've never done that before, but I imagine it's fairly straightforward, once you get the hang of it.

WOMAN: Yes, and you'd be working alongside more experienced staff to begin with, so I'm sure it wouldn't be a problem. The salary's slightly higher here. It's an annual salary of £23,000.

MAN: Right.

WOMAN: I know that if they like you, it's likely you'll be promoted quite quickly. So that's worth thinking about.

MAN: Yes. It does sound interesting. What are the hours like?

WOMAN: The usual, I think. There's a lot of evening and weekend work, but they're closed on Mondays. But you do get one Sunday off every four weeks. So would you like me to send off your … Q10

PART 2

Hello everyone. It's good to see that so many members of the public have shown up for our presentation on the new housing development planned on the outskirts of Nunston. I'm Mark Reynolds and I'm Communications Manager at the development.

I'll start by giving you a brief overview of our plans for the development. So one thing I'm sure you'll want to know is why we've selected this particular site for a housing development. At present it's being used for farming, like much of the land around Nunston. But because of the new industrial centre in Nunston, there's a lot of demand for housing for employees in the region, as many employees are having to commute long distances at present. Of course, there's also the fact that we have an international airport just 20 minutes' drive away, but although that's certainly convenient, it wasn't one of our major criteria for choosing the site. We were more interested in the fact that there's an excellent hospital just 15 kilometres away, and a large secondary school even closer than that. One drawback to the site is that it's on quite a steep slope, but we've taken account of that in our planning so it shouldn't be a major problem. Q11/12 Q11/12

We've had a lot of positive feedback about the plans. People like the wide variety of accommodation types and prices, and the fact that it's only a short drive to get out into the countryside from the development. We were particularly pleased that so many people liked the designs for the layout of the development, with the majority of people saying it generally made a good impression and <u>blended in well with the natural features of the landscape, with provision made for protecting trees and wildlife on the site</u>. Some people have mentioned that they'd like to see more facilities for cyclists, and we'll look at that, but the overall feedback has been that <u>the design and facilities of the development make it seem a place where people of all ages can live together happily</u>.

Q13/14

Q13/14

OK. So I'll put a map of the proposed development up on the screen. You'll see it's bounded on the south side by the main road, which then goes on to Nunston. Another boundary is formed by London Road, on the western side of the development. Inside the development there'll be about 400 houses and 3 apartment blocks.

There'll also be a school for children up to 11 years old. If you look at the South Entrance at the bottom of the map, there's <u>a road from there that goes right up through the development. The school will be on that road, at the corner of the second turning to the left.</u>

Q15

<u>A large sports centre</u> is planned with facilities for indoor and outdoor activities. This will be <u>on the western side of the development, just below the road that branches off from London Road</u>.

Q16

There'll be a clinic where residents can go if they have any health problems. Can you see the lake towards the top of the map? <u>The clinic will be just below this, to the right of a street of houses</u>.

Q17

There'll also be a community centre for people of all ages. <u>On the northeast side of the development, there'll be a row of specially designed houses specifically for residents over 65, and the community centre will be adjoining this</u>.

Q18

We haven't forgotten about shopping. There'll be <u>a supermarket between the two entrances to the development. We're planning to leave the three large trees near London Road, and it'll be just to the south of these</u>.

Q19

It's planned to have a playground for younger children. If you look at <u>the road that goes up from the South Entrance, you'll see it curves round to the left at the top, and the playground will be in that curve, with nice views of the lake</u>.

Q20

OK, so now does anyone …

PART 3

ADAM: So, Michelle, shall we make a start on our presentation? We haven't got that much time left.

MICHELLE: No, Adam. But at least we've done all the background reading. I found it really interesting – I'd never even heard of the Laki eruption before this.

ADAM: Me neither. I suppose 1783 is a long time ago.

MICHELLE: But it was a huge eruption and it had such devastating consequences.

ADAM: I know. It was great there were so many primary sources to look at. It really gives you a sense of how catastrophic the volcano was. People were really trying to make sense of the science for the first time.

MICHELLE: That's right. But <u>what I found more significant was how it impacted directly and indirectly on political events, as well as having massive social and economic consequences</u>.

Q21

ADAM:	I know. That should be the main focus of our presentation.	
MICHELLE:	The observations made by people at the time were interesting, weren't they? I mean, they all gave a pretty consistent account of what happened, even if they didn't always use the same terminology.	
ADAM:	Yeah. <u>I was surprised there were so many weather stations established by that time</u> – so, you know, you can see how the weather changed, often by the hour.	Q22
MICHELLE:	Right. Writers at the time talked about the Laki haze to describe the volcanic fog that spread across Europe. They all realised that this wasn't the sort of fog they were used to – and of course this was in pre-industrial times – so they hadn't experienced sulphur-smelling fog before.	
ADAM:	No, that's true.	
MICHELLE:	Reports from the period <u>blamed the haze for an increase in headaches, respiratory issues and asthma attacks</u>. And they all describe how it covered the sun and made it look a strange red colour.	Q23
ADAM:	Must have been very weird.	
MICHELLE:	It's interesting that Benjamin Franklin wrote about the haze. Did you read that? He was the American ambassador in Paris at the time.	
ADAM:	Yeah. At first no one realised that the haze was caused by the volcanic eruption in Iceland.	
MICHELLE:	<u>It was Benjamin Franklin who realised that before anyone else.</u>	Q24
ADAM:	<u>He's often credited with that, apparently. But a French naturalist beat him to it</u> – I can't remember his name. I'd have to look it up. Then other naturalists had the same idea – all independently of each other.	
MICHELLE:	Oh right. We should talk about the immediate impact of the eruption, which was obviously enormous – especially in Iceland, where so many people died.	
ADAM:	Mmm. You'd expect that – and the fact that the volcanic ash drifted so swiftly – but <u>not that the effects would go on for so long</u>. Or that two years after the eruption, <u>strange weather events were being reported as far away as North America and North Africa.</u>	Q25/26 Q25/26
MICHELLE:	No. I found all that hard to believe too. It must have been terrible – and there was nothing anyone could do about it, even if they knew the ash cloud was coming in their direction.	

MICHELLE:	We should run through some of the terrible consequences of the eruption experienced in different countries. There's quite a varied range.	
ADAM:	Starting with Iceland, where the impact on farming was devastating.	
MICHELLE:	Mmm. One of the most dramatic things there was the effect on <u>livestock as they grazed in the fields. They were poisoned</u> because they ate vegetation that had been contaminated with fluorine as a result of the volcanic fallout.	Q27
ADAM:	That was horrible. In Egypt, the bizarre weather patterns led to a severe drought and as a result the Nile didn't flood, which meant the crops all failed.	
MICHELLE:	It's so far from where the eruption happened and yet <u>the famine there led to more people dying than any other country</u>. It was worse than the plague.	Q28
ADAM:	OK. Then in the UK <u>the mortality rate</u> went up a lot – presumably from respiratory illnesses. According to one report <u>it was about double the usual number and included an unusually high percentage of people under the age of 25</u>.	Q29
MICHELLE:	Mmm. I think people will be surprised to hear that the weather in the USA was badly affected too. George Washington even makes a note in his diary that they were snowbound until March in Virginia. That was before he became president.	
ADAM:	Yes, and <u>there was ice floating down the Mississippi, which was unprecedented</u>.	Q30
MICHELLE:	Astonishing, really. Anyway, what do you think …	

PART 4

Good morning. Now, we've been asked to choose an aspect of European clothing or fashion and to talk about its development over time.

I decided to focus on a rather small area of clothing and that's pockets. I chose pockets for two reasons, really. We all have them – in jeans, jackets, coats, for example – and even though we often carry bags or briefcases as well, <u>nothing is quite as convenient as being able to pop your phone or credit card into your pocket</u>. Yet, I suspect that, other than that, people don't really think about pockets too much and they're rather overlooked as a fashion item.   *Q31*

It's certainly very interesting to go back in time and see how pockets developed for men and women. <u>In the 18th century</u>, fashions were quite different from the way they are now, and   *Q32*
pockets were too. If we think about male fashion first … <u>that was the time when suits became popular</u>. Trousers were knee-length only and referred to as 'breeches', the waistcoats were short and the jackets were long, but <u>all three garments were lined with material and pockets</u>   *Q33*
<u>were sewn into this cloth by whichever tailor the customer used</u>. The wearer could then carry small objects such as pencils or coins on their person and reach them through a gap in the lining. Coat pockets became increasingly decorative on the outside for men who wanted to look stylish, but <u>they were often larger but plainer if the wearer was someone with a</u>   *Q34*
<u>profession who needed to carry medical instruments</u> – a doctor or physician, for example.

The development of women's pockets was a little different. For one thing, <u>they weren't nearly</u>   *Q35*
<u>as visible</u> or as easy to reach as men's. In the 18th and 19th centuries, women carried numerous possessions on their person and some of these could be worth a lot of money. Women were more vulnerable to theft and wealthy women, in particular, worried constantly about pickpockets. So – <u>what they did was to have a pair of pockets made that were tied</u>   *Q36*
<u>together with string</u>. The pockets were made of fabric, which might be recycled cloth if the wearer had little money or something more expensive, such as linen, sometimes featuring very delicate embroidery. <u>Women tied the pockets around their waist</u> so that they hung   *Q37*
beneath their clothes. Remember, skirts were long then and there was plenty of room to hide a whole range of small possessions between the layers of petticoats that were commonly worn. <u>They would have an opening in the folds of their skirts through which they could reach</u>   *Q38*
<u>whatever they needed, like their perfume</u>. Working women, of course, also needed to carry around items that they might use for whatever job or trade they were involved in, but their pairs of pockets still remained on the inside of their clothing, they just got bigger or longer – sometimes reaching down to their knees!

So the tie-on pockets went well into the 19th century and only changed when fashion altered towards the end of that period. That's <u>when dresses became tighter and less bulky, and</u>   *Q39*
<u>the pairs of pockets became very noticeable – they stood out too much and detracted from</u>
<u>the woman's image</u>. Women who had been used to carrying around a range of personal possessions – and still wanted to – needed somewhere to carry these items about their person. That was when small bags, or pouches as they were known, came into fashion and, of course, <u>they inevitably led on to the handbag of more modern times</u>, particularly when   *Q40*
fashion removed pockets altogether.

PART 1

BREDA:	Hello, Wayside Camera Club, Breda speaking.
DAN:	Oh, hello, um, my name's Dan and I'd like to join your club.
BREDA:	That's great, Dan. We have an application form – would you like to complete it over the phone, then you can ask any questions you might have?
DAN:	Oh, yes, thanks.
BREDA:	OK, so what's your family name?
DAN:	It's Green – Dan Green.
BREDA:	So – can I take your email address?
DAN:	Yes, it's dan1068@market.com.
BREDA:	Thanks. And what about your home address?
DAN:	Well, I'm about ten miles away from your club in Peacetown. I live in a house there.
BREDA:	OK, so what's the house number and street?
DAN:	It's 52 <u>Marrowfield Street</u>.
BREDA:	Is that M-A double R-O-W-F-I-E-L-D?
DAN:	That's right.
BREDA:	… and that's Peacetown, you said?
DAN:	Uhuh.

Q1

BREDA:	So how did you hear about our club? Did you look on the internet?
DAN:	I usually do that, but this time, well, <u>I was talking to a relative</u> the other day and he suggested it.
BREDA:	Oh, is he a member too?
DAN:	He belongs to another club – but he'd heard good things about yours.
BREDA:	OK. So what do you hope to get from joining?
DAN:	Well, one thing that really interests me is the competitions that you have. I enjoy entering those.
BREDA:	Right. Anything else?
DAN:	Well, <u>I also like to socialise</u> with other photographers.
BREDA:	That's great. So what type of membership would you like?
DAN:	What are the options?
BREDA:	It's <u>£30 a year for full membership</u> or £20 a year if you're an associate.
DAN:	I think I'll go for the full membership, then.
BREDA:	That's a good idea because you can't vote in meetings with an associate membership.

Q2

Q3

Q4

BREDA:	If I could just find out a bit more about you …
DAN:	OK.
BREDA:	So you said you wanted to compete – have you ever won any photography competitions?
DAN:	Not yet, but I have entered three in the past.
BREDA:	Oh, that's interesting. So why don't you tell me something about those? Let's start with the first one.
DAN:	Well, <u>the theme was entitled 'Domestic Life'</u>.
BREDA:	I see – so it had to be something related to the home?

Q5

DAN:	Yeah. I chose to take a photo of a family sitting round the dinner table having a meal, and, um, I didn't win, but I did get some feedback.
BREDA:	Oh, what did the judges say?
DAN:	That it was too 'busy' as a picture.
BREDA:	Aha – so it was the composition of the picture that they criticised?
DAN:	That's right – and once they'd told me that, I could see my mistake.
BREDA:	So what was the theme of the second competition?
DAN:	Well, my university was on the coast and that area gets a lot of beautiful sunsets, so that was the theme.
BREDA:	Oh, sunsets, that's a great theme.
DAN:	Yes. <u>The instructions were to capture the clouds as well</u> – it couldn't just be blue sky and a setting sun.
BREDA:	Sure, cause they give you all those amazing pinks and purples.
DAN:	Yeah – and I thought I'd done that well, but the feedback was that I should have waited a bit longer to get the shot.
BREDA:	I see. So <u>the timing wasn't right</u>.
DAN:	Yes – I took it too soon, basically. And then <u>the third competition I entered was called 'Animal Magic'</u>.
BREDA:	Well, that's a difficult subject!
DAN:	I know! I had to take hundreds of shots.
BREDA:	I'm sure – because animals move all the time.
DAN:	That's what we had to show – <u>there had to be some movement in the scene</u>. I got a great shot of a fox in the end, but I took it at night and, well, <u>I suspected that it was a bit dark, which is what I was told</u>.
BREDA:	Well Dan – you seem to be really keen and we'd be delighted to have you in our club. I'm sure we can help with all those areas that you've outlined.
DAN:	Thanks, that's great.

Q6 appears beside "The instructions were to capture the clouds as well"
Q7 appears beside "the timing wasn't right"
Q8 appears beside "the third competition I entered was called 'Animal Magic'"
Q9 appears beside "there had to be some movement in the scene"
Q10 appears beside "I suspected that it was a bit dark, which is what I was told"

PART 2

PRESENTER:	This evening we're delighted to welcome Dan Beagle, who's just written a book on looking for and finding food in the wild. He's going to tell us everything we need to know about picking wild mushrooms.
DAN:	Thank you very much. Well, I need to start by talking about safety. You really need to know what you're doing because some mushrooms are extremely poisonous. Having said that, once you know what to look for, it's really worth doing for the amazing variety of mushrooms available – which you can't get in the shops. But of course, you have to be very careful and that's why I always say <u>you should never consume mushrooms picked by friends or neighbours</u> – always remember that some poisonous mushrooms look very similar to edible ones and it's easy for people to get confused. The other thing to <u>avoid is mushrooms growing beside busy</u> roads for obvious reasons. But nothing beats the taste of freshly picked mushrooms – don't forget that the ones in the shops are often several days old and past their best.
	There are certain ideas about wild mushrooms that it's important to be aware of. Don't listen to people who tell you that <u>it's only OK to eat mushrooms that are pale or dull – this is completely untrue. Some edible mushrooms are bright red</u>, for example. Personally, I prefer mushrooms cooked but it won't do you any harm to eat them uncooked in salads – it's not necessary to peel them. Another

Q11/12 appears beside "you should never consume mushrooms picked by friends or neighbours"
Q11/12 appears beside "avoid is mushrooms growing beside busy"
Q13/14 appears beside "it's only OK to eat mushrooms that are pale or dull – this is completely untrue. Some edible mushrooms are bright red"

thing you should remember is that you can't tell if a mushroom is safe to eat by its smell – some of the most deadly mushrooms have no smell and taste quite nice, apparently. Finally, <u>just because deer or squirrels eat a particular mushroom doesn't mean that you can</u>.   *Q13/14*

Of course, mushroom picking is associated with the countryside but if you haven't got a car, your local park can be a great place to start. There are usually a range of habitats where mushrooms grow, such as playing fields and wooded areas. But <u>you need to be there first thing in the morning</u>, as there's likely be a lot of competition – not just from people but wildlife too. The deer often get the best mushrooms in my local park.   *Q15*

If you're a complete beginner, I wouldn't recommend going alone or relying on photos in a book, even the one I've written! There are some really good phone apps for identifying mushrooms, but you can't always rely on getting a good signal in the middle of a wood. <u>If possible, you should go with a group led by an expert</u> – you'll stay safe and learn a lot that way.   *Q16*

Conservation is a really important consideration and you must follow a few basic rules. <u>You should never pick all the mushrooms in one area – collect only enough for your own needs</u>. Be very careful that you don't trample on young mushrooms or other plants. And make sure you don't pick any mushrooms that are endangered and protected by law.   *Q17*

There's been a decline in some varieties of wild mushrooms in this part of the country. Restaurants are becoming more interested in locally sourced food like wild mushrooms, but <u>the biggest problem is that so many new houses have been built in this area in the last ten years</u>. And more water is being taken from rivers and reservoirs because of this, and mushroom habitats have been destroyed.   *Q18*

Anyway, a word of advice on storing mushrooms. Collect them in a brown paper bag and as soon as you get home, put them in the fridge. <u>They'll be fine for a couple of days, but it's best to cook them as soon as possible</u> – after washing them really carefully first, of course.   *Q19*

So everybody knows what a mushroom tastes like, right? Well, you'll be surprised by the huge variety of wild mushrooms there are. Be adventurous! <u>They're great in so many dishes – stir fries, risottos, pasta</u>. But just be aware that some people can react badly to certain varieties so it's a good idea not to eat huge quantities to begin with.   *Q20*

OK, so now I'm going to show you …

PART 3

YOUNG MAN:	That seminar yesterday on automation and the future of work was really good, wasn't it? Looking at the first industrial revolution in Britain in the 19th century and seeing how people reacted to massive change was a real eye-opener.
YOUNG WOMAN:	Yes. It was interesting to hear how people felt about automation then and what challenges they faced. I didn't know that first started with workers in the textile industry.
YOUNG MAN:	With those protesting workers called the Luddites destroying their knitting machines because they were so worried about losing their jobs.

YOUNG WOMAN:	Yes, and <u>ultimately, they didn't achieve anything</u>. And anyway, industrialisation created more jobs than it destroyed.	*Q21/22*
YOUNG MAN:	Yes, that's true – but <u>it probably didn't seem a positive thing at the time. I can see why the Luddites felt so threatened</u>.	*Q21/22*
YOUNG WOMAN:	I know. I'm sure I would have felt the same. The discussion about the future of work was really optimistic for a change. I like the idea that work won't involve doing boring, repetitive tasks, as robots will do all that. Normally, you only hear negative stuff about the future.	
YOUNG MAN:	Bit too optimistic, don't you think? For example, I can't see how people are about to have more leisure time, when <u>all the evidence shows people are spending longer than ever at work</u>.	*Q23/24*
YOUNG WOMAN:	No – that's true. And what about <u>lower unemployment? I'm not so sure about that</u>.	*Q23/24*
YOUNG MAN:	Perhaps in the long term – but not in the foreseeable future.	
YOUNG WOMAN:	Mmm. And I expect most people will be expected to work until they're much older – as everyone's living much longer.	
YOUNG MAN:	That's already happening.	

YOUNG WOMAN:	I enjoyed all that stuff on how technology has changed some jobs and how they're likely to change in the near future.	
YOUNG MAN:	Yeah, incredible. Like accountants. You might think all the technological innovations would have put them out of a job, but in fact <u>there are more of them than ever. They're still really in demand and have become far more efficient</u>.	*Q25*
YOUNG WOMAN:	Right. That was amazing. Twenty times more accountants in this country compared to the 19th century.	
YOUNG MAN:	I know. I'd never have thought that demand for hairdressing would have gone up so much in the last hundred years. One hairdresser for every 287 people now, compared to one for over 1,500.	
YOUNG WOMAN:	Yeah because <u>people's earning power has gone up so they can afford to spend more on personal services like that</u>.	*Q26*
YOUNG MAN:	But technology hasn't changed the actual job that much.	
YOUNG WOMAN:	No, they've got hairdryers, etc. but it's one job where you don't depend on a computer … The kind of work that administrative staff do has changed enormously, thanks to technology. Even 20 years ago there were secretaries doing dictation and typing.	
YOUNG MAN:	Yes. <u>Really boring compared to these days, when they're given much more responsibility and higher status</u>.	*Q27*
YOUNG WOMAN:	Mmm. A lot of graduates go in for this kind of work now … I'd expected there to be a much bigger change in the number of agricultural workers in the 19th century. But the 1871 census showed that roughly 25% of the population worked on the land.	
YOUNG MAN:	Yeah, <u>I'd have assumed it would be more than 50%. Now it's less than 0.2%</u>.	*Q28*
YOUNG WOMAN:	What about care workers?	
YOUNG MAN:	They barely existed in the 19th century as people's lifespan was so much shorter. <u>But now of course this sector will see huge growth</u>.	*Q29*
YOUNG WOMAN:	Yeah – and it's hard enough to meet current demand. The future looks quite bleak for bank clerks. They've been in decline since ATMs were introduced in the eighties.	
YOUNG MAN:	And <u>technology will certainly make most of the jobs they do now redundant</u>, I think.	*Q30*
YOUNG WOMAN:	I agree, although the situation may change. It's very hard to predict what will happen.	

PART 4

In today's astronomy lecture, I'm going to talk about the need for a system to manage the movement of satellites and other objects in orbit around the Earth. In other words, a Space Traffic Management system. We already have effective Air Traffic Control systems that are used internationally to ensure that planes navigate our skies safely. Well, Space Traffic Management is a similar concept, but focusing on the control of satellites.

The aim of such a system would be to prevent the danger of collisions in space between the objects in orbit around the Earth. In order to do this, we'd need to have a set of legal measures, and we'd also have to develop the technical systems to enable us to prevent such accidents.   *Q31*

But unfortunately, at present we don't actually have a Space Traffic Management system that works. So why not? What are the problems in developing such a system?

Well, for one thing, satellites are relatively cheap these days, compared with how they were in the past, meaning that more people can afford to put them into space. So there's a lot more of them out there, and people aren't just launching single satellites but whole constellations, consisting of thousands of them designed to work together. So space is getting more crowded every day.   *Q32*   *Q33*

But in spite of this, one thing you may be surprised to learn is that you can launch a satellite into space and, once it's out there, it doesn't have to send back any information to Earth to allow its identification. So while we have international systems for ensuring we know where the *planes* in our skies are, and to prevent them from colliding with one another, when it comes to the safety of *satellites*, at present we don't have anything like enough proper ways of tracking them.   *Q34*   *Q35*

And it isn't just entire satellites that we need to consider. A greater threat is the huge amount of space debris in orbit around the Earth – broken bits of satellite and junk from space stations and so on. And some of these are so small that they can be very hard to identify, but they can still be very dangerous.

In addition, some operators may be unwilling to share information about the satellites they've launched. For example, a satellite may be designed for military purposes, or it may have been launched for commercial reasons, and the operators don't want competitors to have information about it.   *Q36*

And even if the operators *are* willing to provide it, the information isn't easy to collect. Details are needed about the object itself, as well as about its location at a particular time – and remember that a satellite isn't very big, and it's likely to be moving at thousands of kilometres an hour. We don't have any sensors that can constantly follow something moving so fast, so all that the scientists can do is to put forward a prediction concerning where the satellite is heading next.   *Q37*   *Q38*

So those are some of the problems that we're facing. Let's consider now some of the solutions that have been suggested. One key issue is the way in which information is dealt with. We need more information, but it also needs to be accessible at a global level, so we need to establish shared standards that we can all agree on for the way in which this information is presented. We already do this in other areas of science, so although this is a challenge, it's not an impossible task. Then, as all this information's collected, it needs to be put together so it can be used, and that will involve creating a single database on which it can be entered.   *Q39*

As we continue to push forward new developments, congestion of the space environment is only going to increase. To cope with this, we need to develop a system like the one I've described to coordinate the work of the numerous spacecraft operators, but it's also essential that this system is one that establishes *trust* in the people that use it, both nationally and at a global level.   *Q40*

One interesting development …

TEST 4

PART 1

JULIE:	Hello?
GREG:	Oh, hello. Is that Julie Davison?
JULIE:	Yes.
GREG:	This is Greg Preston from the Employment Agency. We met last week when you came in to enquire about office work.
JULIE:	Oh, that's right.
GREG:	Now we've just had some details come in of a job which might interest you.
JULIE:	OK.
GREG:	So this is <u>a position for a receptionist</u> – I believe you've done that sort of work before?
JULIE:	Yes, I have, I worked in a sports centre for a couple of years before I got married and had the children.
GREG:	Right. Well, this job's in <u>Fordham, so not too far away for you, and it's at the medical centre there.</u>
JULIE:	OK. So where exactly is that?
GREG:	It's quite near the station, on <u>Chastons Road</u>.
JULIE:	Sorry?
GREG:	Chastons Road – that's C-H-A–S-T-O-N-S.
JULIE:	OK, thanks. So what would the work involve? Dealing with enquiries from patients?
GREG:	Yes, and you'd also be involved in <u>making appointments</u>, whether face to face or on the phone. And rescheduling them if necessary.
JULIE:	Fine, that shouldn't be a problem.
GREG:	And another of your duties would be <u>keeping the centre's database up-to-date</u>. Then you might have other general administrative duties as well, but those would be the main ones.
JULIE:	OK.
GREG:	Now when the details came in, I immediately thought of you because <u>one thing they do require is someone with experience</u>, and you did mention your work at the sports centre when you came in to see us.
JULIE:	Yes, in fact I enjoyed that job. Is there anything else they're looking for?
GREG:	Well, they say it's quite a high-pressure environment, they're always very busy, and patients are often under stress, so they want someone who can cope with that and <u>stay calm, and at the same time be confident</u> when interacting with the public.
JULIE:	Well, after dealing with three children all under five, I reckon I can cope with that.
GREG:	I'm sure you can.
GREG:	And then another thing they mention is that they're looking for someone with good IT skills …
JULIE:	Not a problem.
GREG:	So you'd be interested in following this up?
JULIE:	Sure. When would it start?
GREG:	Well, they're looking for someone from the beginning of next month, but I should tell you that <u>this isn't a permanent job, it's temporary</u>, so the contract would be just to the end of September. But they do say that there could be further opportunities after that.
JULIE:	OK. And what would the hours be?

Q1

Q2

Q3

Q4

Q5

Q6

Q7

Q8

GREG:	Well, they want someone who can start at a quarter to eight in the morning – could you manage that?	
JULIE:	Yes, my husband would have to get the kids up and off to my mother's – she's going to be looking after them while I'm at work. What time would I finish?	
GREG:	<u>One fifteen.</u>	*Q9*
JULIE:	That should work out all right. I can pick the kids up on my way home, and then I'll have the afternoon with them. Oh, one thing … <u>is there parking available for staff at the centre</u>?	*Q10*
GREG:	<u>Yes, there is</u>, and it's also on a bus route.	
JULIE:	Right. Well, I expect I'll have the car but it's good to know that. OK, so where do I go from here?	
GREG:	Well, if you're happy for me to do so, I'll forward your CV and references, and then the best thing would probably be for you to phone them so they can arrange for an interview.	
JULIE:	Great. Well thank you very much.	
GREG:	You're welcome. Bye now.	
JULIE:	Bye.	

PART 2

Good morning everyone, and welcome to the Museum of Farming Life. I understand it's your first visit here, so I'd like to give you some background information about the museum and then explain a little about what you can see during your visit.

So, where we're standing at the moment is the entrance to a large building that was <u>constructed in 1880 as the home of a local businessman</u>, Alfred Palmer, of the Palmer biscuit factory. It was later sold and became a hall of residence for students in 1911, and a museum in 1951. In 2005, a modern extension was built to accommodate the museum's collections.   *Q11*

The museum's owned by the university, and apart from two rooms that are our offices, the university <u>uses the main part of the building. You may see students going into the building for lessons</u>, but it's not open to museum visitors, I'm afraid. It's a shame because the interior architectural features are outstanding, especially the room that used to be the library.   *Q12*

Luckily, we've managed to keep entry to the museum free. This includes access to all the galleries, outdoor areas and the rooms for special exhibitions. We run activities for children and students, such as the museum club, for which there's no charge. <u>We do have a donation box just over there so feel free to give whatever amount you consider appropriate.</u>   *Q13*

We do have <u>a cloakroom, if you'd like to leave your coats and bags somewhere</u>. Unlike other museums, photography is allowed here, so you might like to keep your cameras with you. You might be more comfortable not carrying around heavy rucksacks, <u>though keep your coats and jackets on as it's quite cold in the museum garden today</u>.   *Q14*

I'd like to tell you about the different areas of the museum.

Just inside, and outside the main gallery, we have an area called Four Seasons. Here you can watch a four-minute animation of a woodland scene. <u>It was designed especially for the museum by a group of young people on a film studies course</u>, and it's beautiful. Children absolutely love it, but then, so do adults.   *Q15*

The main gallery's called Town and Country. It includes a photographic collection of prize-winning sheep and shepherds. Leaving Town and Country, you enter Farmhouse Kitchen, which is … well, self-explanatory. Here we have the oldest collection of equipment for making

butter and cheese in the country. And <u>this morning, a specialist cheesemaker will be giving</u>   *Q16*
<u>demonstrations</u> of how it's produced. You may even get to try some.

After that, you can go in two directions. To the right is a staircase that takes you up to a landing from where you can look down on the galleries. To the left is a room called A Year on the Farm. There's lots of seating here as sometimes we use the room for school visits, so it's a good place to stop for a rest. <u>If you're feeling competitive, you can take our memory test in</u>   *Q17*
<u>which you answer questions about things you've seen in the museum</u>.

The next area's called Wagon Walk. This contains farm carts from nearly every part of the country. It's surprising how much regional variation there was. Beside the carts are display boards with information about each one. <u>The carts are old and fragile, so we ask you to keep</u>   *Q18*
<u>your children close to you and ensure they don't climb on the carts</u>.

From Wagon Walk, you can either make your way back to reception or go out into the garden – or even go back to take another look in the galleries. In the far corner of the garden is Bees are Magic, but <u>we're redeveloping this area so you can't visit that at the moment</u>. You can still   *Q19*
buy our honey in the shop, though.

Finally, there's The Pond, which contains all kinds of interesting wildlife. <u>There are baby</u>   *Q20*
<u>ducks that are only a few days old, as well as tiny frogs</u>. The Pond isn't deep and there's a fence around it, so it's perfectly safe for children.

PART 3

TUTOR:	So now I want you to discuss the lesson we've just been watching on the video and think about the ways in which origami can be a useful educational tool. Can you all work with the person sitting next to you …
SEB:	I had no idea that such a simple thing like folding squares of paper to make the shape of something like a bird could be such an amazing tool. It's made me see origami in a whole new light.
LIA:	I know. It was interesting to see the educational skills the children were developing by doing origami. On the video you could see them really <u>listening hard to make sure they did all the steps in the right order</u> to make the bird.
SEB:	That's right. In this lesson they were working individually but it would also be interesting to see if the children could work out how to make something simple without being given any direction. That would help with building teamwork as well.
LIA:	Yes, but much more of a challenge. One thing that really stood out for me was that <u>the children were all having fun while being taught</u> something new.
SEB:	Which is a key aim of any lesson with this age group. And although these kids had no problems with folding the paper, with younger children you could do origami to help practise fine motor skills.
LIA:	Absolutely. Shall we talk about the individual children we saw on the video? I wrote all their names down and took some notes.
SEB:	Yes, I did too.
LIA:	OK, good. Let's start with Sid.
SEB:	He was interesting because before they started doing the origami, he was being quite disruptive.
LIA:	Yes. He really benefited from having to use his hands – <u>it helped him to settle down and start concentrating</u>.

Q21/22 (beside Lia's listening comment)

Q21/22 (beside Lia's "having fun" comment)

Q23 (beside Lia's final comment)

SEB:	Yes, I noticed that too. What about Jack? I noticed he seemed to want to work things out for himself.	
LIA:	Mmm. <u>You could see him trying out different things rather than asking the teacher for help.</u> What did you make of Naomi?	Q24
SEB:	She seemed to be losing interest at one point but then <u>she decided she wanted her mouse to be the best and that motivated her to try harder.</u>	Q25
LIA:	She didn't seem satisfied with hers in the end, though.	
SEB:	No.	
LIA:	Anya was such a star. She listened so carefully and then <u>produced the perfect bird with very little effort.</u>	Q26
SEB:	Mmm – I think the teacher could have increased the level of difficulty for her.	
LIA:	Maybe. I think it was the first time Zara had come across origami.	
SEB:	She looked as if she didn't really get what was going on.	
LIA:	<u>She seemed unsure about what she was supposed to do,</u> but in the end hers didn't turn out too badly.	Q27
SEB:	Yeah. I'm sure it was a positive learning experience for her.	
LIA:	Mmm.	

LIA:	I think one reason why the origami activity worked so well in this class was that the teacher was well prepared.	
SEB:	Right. I think it would have taken me ages to <u>prepare examples, showing each of the steps involved in making the bird. But that was a really good idea.</u> The children could see what they were aiming for – and much better for them to be able to hold something, rather than just looking at pictures.	Q28
LIA:	Mmm – those physical examples supported her verbal explanations really well.	
SEB:	It's strange that origami isn't used more widely. Why do you think that is?	
LIA:	Well, teachers may just feel it's not that appealing to children who are used to doing everything on computers, especially boys. Even if they're aware of the benefits.	
SEB:	Oh, I don't know. It's no different to any other craft activity. <u>I bet it's because so many teachers are clumsy like me.</u>	Q29
LIA:	<u>That's true – too much effort required if you're not good with your hands.</u>	
SEB:	Well, anyway, <u>I think we should try it out in our maths teaching practice with Year 3.</u> I can see using origami is a really engaging way of reinforcing children's knowledge of geometric shapes, like they were doing in the video, but <u>I think it would also work really well for presenting fractions, which is coming up soon.</u>	Q30
LIA:	Good idea – that's something most of the kids in that class might struggle with. Origami would also be good practice for using symmetry – but I think they did that last term.	
SEB:	OK – well let's try and get some ideas together and plan the lesson next week.	
TUTOR:	OK, if you could all stop …	

PART 4

The person I've chosen to talk about is the French writer Victor Hugo – many people have heard of him because his novel, *Les Misérables*, which he wrote in 1862, is famous around the world. It became a stage musical in the 1980s, and a film version was also released in 2012. So, <u>some of us, I'm sure, have a pretty general idea of the plot, but we know much less about the author.</u> Today, I'm going to provide a little more insight into this talented man and I'm going to talk particularly about the home he had on the island of Guernsey in the British Channel Islands.

Q31

But first, his early career ... as I've said, he was a writer, he was at the height of his career in Paris and he was very highly regarded by his colleagues. As far as literature was concerned, he was the leading figure of the Romantic movement. However, as well as being a literary genius, <u>he also gave many speeches about issues like the level of poverty</u> in his society. He felt very strongly about this and about other areas where change was needed, like education. This kind of outspoken criticism was not well liked by the rulers of France and, eventually, the emperor – Napoleon III – told Victor Hugo to leave Paris and not return; in other words, he sent him into exile.

Q32

So <u>Victor Hugo was forced to reside in other parts of Europe</u>. Guernsey was actually his third place of exile and he landed there in 1855. He produced a lot while on Guernsey – including *Les Misérables* – and to do this, he had to spend a great deal of time in the home that he had there. This was a property that <u>he bought using the money he'd made in France from the publication of a collection of his poetry</u>. It was the only property he ever owned, and he was very proud of it.

Q33

Q34

The property Victor Hugo bought on Guernsey was a large, five-storey house in the capital town of St Peter Port and he lived there for 15 years, returning to France in 1870 when Napoleon's Empire collapsed. He decorated and furnished each level, or floor, of the house in unique and wonderful ways, and many people consider the inside of the house to be a 'work of art'. Today it's a museum that attracts 200,000 visitors a year.

He lived in the house with his family ... and <u>portraits of its members still hang in rooms on the ground floor, along with drawings</u> that he did during his travels that he felt were important to him. In other ground-floor rooms, there are huge tapestries that he would have designed and loved. <u>The walls are covered in dark wood panelling that Victor Hugo created himself using wooden furniture that he bought in the market</u>. The items were relatively inexpensive, and he used them to create intricate carvings. They gave an atmosphere on the lower level that was shadowy and rather solemn.

Q35

Q36

On the next level of the house there are two impressive lounges, where he entertained his guests. One lounge has entirely red furnishings, such as sofas and wall coverings, and the other blue. <u>There's a strong Chinese influence in these areas in things like the wallpaper pattern and the lamps</u> – which he would have made himself by copying original versions.

Q37

His library, where he left many of his favourite books, forms the hallway to the third floor and was a comfortable area where he could relax and enjoy his afternoons. And then, at the very top of the house, <u>there's a room called the Lookout – called that because it looks out over the harbour</u>. In contrast to the rather dark lower levels, it's full of light and was like a glass office where he would write until lunchtime – often at his desk.

Q38

So, Victor Hugo was a man of many talents, but he was also true to his values. While living in his house on Guernsey, he entertained many other famous writers, but <u>he also invited a large group of local children from the deprived areas of the island to dinner once a week</u>. What's more, he served them their food, which was an extraordinary gesture for the time period.

Q39

In 1927, <u>the house was owned by his relatives, and they decided to donate it to the city of Paris</u>. It has since been restored using photographs from the period and, as I mentioned earlier, is now a museum that is open to the public.

Q40

Listening and Reading answer keys

TEST 1

LISTENING

 Answer key with extra explanations in Resource Bank

Part 1, Questions 1–10

1 DW30 7YZ
2 24(th) April
3 dentist
4 parking
5 Claxby
6 late
7 evening
8 supermarket
9 pollution
10 storage

Part 2, Questions 11–20

11 C
12 A
13 A
14&15 *IN EITHER ORDER*
    B
    E
16 B
17 G
18 D
19 A
20 F

Part 3, Questions 21–30

21 A
22 B
23 A
24 C
25 B
26 A
27&28 *IN EITHER ORDER*
    B
    E
29&30 *IN EITHER ORDER*
    A
    C

Part 4, Questions 31–40

31 fences
32 family
33 helicopters
34 stress
35 sides
36 breathing
37 feet
38 employment
39 weapons
40 tourism

If you score …

0–19	20–28	29–40
you are unlikely to get an acceptable score under examination conditions and we recommend that you spend a lot of time improving your English before you take IELTS.	you may get an acceptable score under examination conditions but we recommend that you think about having more practice or lessons before you take IELTS.	you are likely to get an acceptable score under examination conditions but remember that different institutions will find different scores acceptable.

TEST 1

READING

 Answer key with extra explanations in Resource Bank

Reading Passage 1, Questions 1–13

1 lettuces
2 1,000 kg
3 (food) consumption
4 pesticides
5 journeys
6 producers
7 flavour / flavor
8 TRUE
9 NOT GIVEN
10 FALSE
11 TRUE
12 FALSE
13 NOT GIVEN

Reading Passage 2, Questions 14–26

14 B
15 A
16 C
17 E
18 B
19 B
20 C

21 C
22 fire
23 nutrients
24 cavities
25 hawthorn
26 rare

Reading Passage 3, Questions 27–40

27 C
28 F
29 A
30 E
31 B
32 sustainability
33 fuel
34 explosions
35 bankrupt
36 C
37 D
38 B
39 D
40 A

If you score ...

0–17	18–26	27–40
you are unlikely to get an acceptable score under examination conditions and we recommend that you spend a lot of time improving your English before you take IELTS.	you may get an acceptable score under examination conditions but we recommend that you think about having more practice or lessons before you take IELTS.	you are likely to get an acceptable score under examination conditions but remember that different institutions will find different scores acceptable.

TEST 2

LISTENING

 Answer key with extra explanations in Resource Bank

Part 1, Questions 1–10

1 training
2 discount
3 taxi
4 service
5 English
6 Wivenhoe
7 equipment
8 9.75
9 deliveries
10 Sunday

Part 2, Questions 11–20

11&12 *IN EITHER ORDER*
B
E
13&14 *IN EITHER ORDER*
B
C
15 G
16 C
17 D
18 B
19 H
20 A

Part 3, Questions 21–30

21 C
22 A
23 B
24 B
25&26 *IN EITHER ORDER*
A
B
27 D
28 A
29 C
30 F

Part 4, Questions 31–40

31 convenient
32 suits
33 tailor
34 profession
35 visible
36 string(s)
37 waist(s)
38 perfume
39 image
40 handbag

If you score …

0–18	19–28	29–40
you are unlikely to get an acceptable score under examination conditions and we recommend that you spend a lot of time improving your English before you take IELTS.	you may get an acceptable score under examination conditions but we recommend that you think about having more practice or lessons before you take IELTS.	you are likely to get an acceptable score under examination conditions but remember that different institutions will find different scores acceptable.

TEST 2

READING

 Answer key with extra explanations in Resource Bank

Reading Passage 1, Questions 1–13

1	(deer) antlers
2	(timber) posts
3	tree trunks
4	oxen
5	glaciers
6	druids
7	burial
8	calendar
9	TRUE
10	FALSE
11	FALSE
12	TRUE
13	NOT GIVEN

Reading Passage 2, Questions 14–26

14	C
15	A
16	B
17	D
18	C
19	D
20	YES
21	NOT GIVEN
22	NO
23	YES
24	C
25	A
26	E

Reading Passage 3, Questions 27–40

27	NOT GIVEN
28	NOT GIVEN
29	TRUE
30	FALSE
31	TRUE
32	NOT GIVEN
33	FALSE
34	transport
35	staircases
36	engineering
37	rule
38	Roman
39	Paris
40	outwards

If you score ...

0–17	18–26	27–40
you are unlikely to get an acceptable score under examination conditions and we recommend that you spend a lot of time improving your English before you take IELTS.	you may get an acceptable score under examination conditions but we recommend that you think about having more practice or lessons before you take IELTS.	you are likely to get an acceptable score under examination conditions but remember that different institutions will find different scores acceptable.

TEST 3

LISTENING

 Answer key with extra explanations in Resource Bank

Part 1, Questions 1–10

1 Marrowfield
2 relative
3 socialise / socialize
4 full
5 Domestic Life
6 clouds
7 timing
8 Animal Magic
9 (animal) movement
10 dark

Part 2, Questions 11–20

11&12 *IN EITHER ORDER*
    B
    C
13&14 *IN EITHER ORDER*
    B
    D
15 C
16 B
17 B
18 C
19 A
20 A

Part 3, Questions 21–30

21&22 *IN EITHER ORDER*
    A
    E
23&24 *IN EITHER ORDER*
    B
    D
25 G
26 E
27 B
28 C
29 F
30 A

Part 4, Questions 31–40

31 technical
32 cheap
33 thousands
34 identification
35 tracking
36 military
37 location
38 prediction
39 database
40 trust

If you score …

0–18	19–28	29–40
you are unlikely to get an acceptable score under examination conditions and we recommend that you spend a lot of time improving your English before you take IELTS.	you may get an acceptable score under examination conditions but we recommend that you think about having more practice or lessons before you take IELTS.	you are likely to get an acceptable score under examination conditions but remember that different institutions will find different scores acceptable.

TEST 3

READING

 Answer key with extra explanations
in Resource Bank

Reading Passage 1,
Questions 1–13

1	G
2	D
3	C
4	F
5	architects
6	moisture
7	layers
8	speed
9	C
10	A
11	B
12	D
13	A

Reading Passage 2,
Questions 14–26

14	iii
15	viii
16	vi
17	v
18	vii
19	i
20	iv

21	A
22	C
23	B
24	speed
25	fifty / 50
26	strict

Reading Passage 3,
Questions 27–40

27	B
28	A
29	C
30	C
31	H
32	D
33	F
34	E
35	B
36	NO
37	NOT GIVEN
38	YES
39	NO
40	NOT GIVEN

If you score …

0–17	18–26	27–40
you are unlikely to get an acceptable score under examination conditions and we recommend that you spend a lot of time improving your English before you take IELTS.	you may get an acceptable score under examination conditions but we recommend that you think about having more practice or lessons before you take IELTS.	you are likely to get an acceptable score under examination conditions but remember that different institutions will find different scores acceptable.

TEST 4

LISTENING

 Answer key with extra explanations in Resource Bank

Part 1, Questions 1–10

1 receptionist
2 Medical
3 Chastons
4 appointments
5 database
6 experience
7 confident
8 temporary
9 1.15
10 parking

Part 2, Questions 11–20

11 B
12 A
13 A
14 C
15 F
16 G
17 E
18 A
19 C
20 B

Part 3, Questions 21–30

21&22 *IN EITHER ORDER*
    B
    D
23 D
24 A
25 C
26 G
27 F
28 A
29 B
30 C

Part 4, Questions 31–40

31 plot
32 poverty
33 Europe
34 poetry
35 drawings
36 furniture
37 lamps
38 harbour / harbor
39 children
40 relatives

If you score …

0–17	18–27	28–40
you are unlikely to get an acceptable score under examination conditions and we recommend that you spend a lot of time improving your English before you take IELTS.	you may get an acceptable score under examination conditions but we recommend that you think about having more practice or lessons before you take IELTS.	you are likely to get an acceptable score under examination conditions but remember that different institutions will find different scores acceptable.

TEST 4

READING

 Answer key with extra explanations in Resource Bank

Reading Passage 1, Questions 1–13

1	D
2	C
3	E
4	B
5	D
6	energy
7	food
8	gardening
9	obesity
10&11	*IN EITHER ORDER*
	C
	D
12&13	*IN EITHER ORDER*
	A
	D

Reading Passage 2, Questions 14–26

14	B
15	C
16	D
17	C
18	B
19	A
20	E
21	B
22	D
23	YES
24	NO
25	NOT GIVEN
26	YES

Reading Passage 3, Questions 27–40

27	YES
28	NOT GIVEN
29	NO
30	NO
31	I
32	F
33	A
34	C
35	H
36	E
37	B
38	A
39	D
40	C

If you score …

0–17	18–26	27–40
you are unlikely to get an acceptable score under examination conditions and we recommend that you spend a lot of time improving your English before you take IELTS.	you may get an acceptable score under examination conditions but we recommend that you think about having more practice or lessons before you take IELTS.	you are likely to get an acceptable score under examination conditions but remember that different institutions will find different scores acceptable.

Sample Writing answers

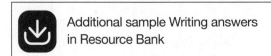

Additional sample Writing answers in Resource Bank

TEST 1, WRITING TASK 1

This is an answer written by a candidate who achieved a **Band 6.0** score.

The line graph illustrates the proportion of urban citizens in Philippines, Malaysia, Thailand and Indonesia between 1970 and 2020, with the expected population in 2030 and 2040.

Overall, it can be easily seen that all four countries has a dramatic rise in population, starting at the lowest point in 1970 and being projected to reach the peak in 2040.

Malaysia and Indonesia saw a slightly rise in population, respectively from 30 to about 45 and around 12 to over 20 percent from 1970 to 1990. After that, both countries has climbed rapidly until now before being predicted to continue increasing for the next 20 years.

After almost remaining in the 70s, Philippines percentage increased dramatically to reach about 47 percent on 1990 and dropped to 40% in 2010. Then, this country faced slightly rise in 2020. Meanwhile, Thailand reached approximate 30% in 1990 and saw not much changes until 2020. Both two countries are projected to increase in population in 2030 and 2040.

Here is the examiner's comment:

> This response covers the requirements of the task. There is an overview in the second paragraph and key features are presented for each country, with main trends identified.

> Ideas are grouped together with a clear overall progression: countries with a similar trend are presented in the same paragraph, first Malaysia and Indonesia, then Thailand and the Philippines. There is some effective use of linkers [*Overall* | *After that* | *Meanwhile*] and other cohesive devices [*respectively* | *this country*], but a few errors remain [*Both two*].

> Vocabulary includes a range, with some less common examples [*proportion* | *expected population* | *dramatic rise* | *projected to reach the peak*]. There are some errors [*slightly* / slight | *almost remaining* | *approximate* / approximately], which do not impede communication.

> The mix of grammatical structures is good, with some complex sentence forms [*being predicted to continue increasing for the next 20 years*]. Some errors remain, but they rarely reduce communication.

> To improve the Band Score for this response, there could be more detail on the similarity of the trends on the graph, more detail on data from 1990 onwards and fewer errors in spelling and grammar. However, this is a good response that does address the requirements of the task.

TEST 1, WRITING TASK 2

This model has been prepared by an examiner as an example of a very good answer.

Scientific developments are occurring at a great rate but some of them do not seem to be of help to people. In fact, sometimes scientific innovations are regretted by those who invented them. This essay will argue that science should never harm people but scientists should aim to further their understanding as much as to improve people's lives.

On one hand, there is a strong argument that the public good should be the top priority for scientists. They are the ones who have the potential to make discoveries and invent things that can change the world. Electricity, modern medicine, telecommunications and the internet are just some of the scientific innovations that have changed lives for the better.

On the other hand, sometimes scientists do research just in the hope of adding to their knowledge. While they should make absolutely sure that their experiments do no harm, they may not know until they have finished how their findings will be used and whether they will improve people's lives. The scientist Nobel invented dynamite to help with mining, not knowing that it would one day be used in weapons, and the scientist who discovered the life-saving drug penicillin did so quite by chance.

Overall, it seems that science should improve the lives of people and that ought to be one of its aims. However, knowledge and discovery are aims in themselves and are just as important for scientists. Sometimes scientists do not know how their scientific breakthroughs will be used until their work is done.

Here are comments from another examiner:

> This response presents a well-developed response to the question and concludes that the aim of scientific discoveries should be to improve people's lives, but that the process often results in unexpected outcomes.

> The candidate agrees with but adds to the statement. This is acceptable in a 'to what extent' question, as the candidate is explaining that the extent cannot always be predicted.

> The candidate presents the argument that the true aim of science is gaining new knowledge and discoveries. They agree that this should be to improve people's lives but that the results can't be predicted.

> The second paragraph gives examples of discoveries that have changed people's lives for the better [*Electricity, modern medicine, telecommunications and the internet*].

> To improve the response, this paragraph could be expanded so that the list of discoveries is fully aligned with the question.

The third paragraph presents the other side, that scientists do not often know what they will find. Examples of two innovations are given [*dynamite* | *penicillin*] to support this point.

Ideas are logically organised and paragraphs have clear central topics. Cohesive devices are used appropriately with some appropriate referencing [*them* | *their* | *it*], although linkers often appear at the start of the sentence, which can seem a little mechanical [*On one hand* | *On the other hand* | *While* | *Overall* | *However* | *Sometimes*].

In order to improve the overall rating, the second paragraph could be further extended and the use of cohesive devices could be less mechanical and not always at the start of each sentence.

However, this is a strong, higher-level response to the task.

TEST 2, WRITING TASK 1

This is an answer written by a candidate who achieved a **Band 5.5** score.

The graph illustrats the data of different levels of annual wage of families in the united states in 2007, 2011 and 2015.

As far as the number of families whose annual income was less than $25,000, it began with around >5 million in 2007, then increased to approximately 27 million in 2011, but decreased by 2 million 4 years later. Similarly, those of families that earned $25,000 to $49,999 were about 25 million in 2007, after that it rose to nearly 30 million in 2011. Finally it decreased to around 27 million in 2015.

By contrast, the groups of families which have high income, including $75,000 to $99,999 and $100,000 or more, experienced a drop in 2011, but their data went up in 2015.

Interesting things could be seen in the group of middle income, the data remain the same in 2007, 2011 and 2015.

Here is the examiner's comment:

> This response does present most of the data within the bar chart and the key features required.
>
> To improve the response, an overview of the information should be included, for example: Across the 8 years, households with incomes below $50,000 rose, then fell back slightly, households with incomes of over $75,000 fell slightly then increased and those with the mid-level incomes remained the same.
>
> The information is arranged coherently, starting with the details for the lower-income households, then the higher, then the mid-section. There are some effective cohesive devices [*As far as | Similarly | By contrast*].
>
> The vocabulary is suitable for the task, but there is an error [>5 *million* / 25 million] which is not helpful when reporting the details.
>
> There is a mix of simple and complex structures, with sentences that contain multiple clauses. There are some examples of missing capitalisation [*united states* / United States] with some errors [*remain* / remained].
>
> To improve the response, it is important to re-read to check for small errors with vocabulary and to include an overview or summary of the salient information.

TEST 2, WRITING TASK 2

This model has been prepared by an examiner as an example of a very good answer.

Students attend university to improve their prospects and find suitable employment after graduation. For this reason, some feel that they should focus all their energy on their main subjects to gain a relevant qualification. Others want a more well-rounded education, so they try to learn about additional subjects.

It is perfectly reasonable for students to enter university with a strong sense of curiosity and a desire to learn as much as possible. Unfortunately, we tend to put subjects into artificial boxes, suggesting that business, art and science are not connected. If students become too focused on a single area, it may stifle their initial curiosity, limiting their potential. They could also graduate with a very narrow skill set that doesn't translate well to the current job market, which often favours those who have taken a multidisciplinary approach to their studies.

Despite this, caution is certainly needed. The more we learn about a subject, the more complex it becomes. Gaining an in-depth, specialist knowledge of a subject requires a certain level of focus and dedication over a long period. If we try to learn about too many things at once, our knowledge may lack the depth required to obtain a qualification. If they are not careful, young people could begin to lose interest in their main subjects, which would be detrimental to their studies.

While learning about other subjects is not necessarily a bad thing, I believe university students should ensure that their main subjects remain the priority so that they do not lose sight of their objective: gaining a qualification. Then they can calculate how much time, energy and headspace they have left for learning about other topics.

Here are comments from another examiner:

> This response addresses both parts of the task and presents a clear opinion at the end. The second paragraph explains how the current university system is set up to [*put subjects into artificial boxes*] and how this narrow focus can disadvantage students. The third paragraph presents the benefits of [*Gaining an in-depth, specialist knowledge*] and the dangers of trying to include too much. Both sides of the question are addressed in well-developed paragraphs.

> To improve the response, it would be helpful to set out the opinion at the start, for added continuity of the position.

> Vocabulary is natural and sophisticated [*stifle their initial curiosity* | *Gaining an in-depth, specialist knowledge* | *detrimental to their studies*] without errors.

> Grammatical structures are wide-ranging, with a range of tenses and conditional [*if*] and modal [*may* | *could* | *would* | *can*] structures embedded in complex, flexible sentences.

> This is a high-level response which fully addresses the task.

TEST 3, WRITING TASK 1

This model has been prepared by an examiner as an example of a very good answer.

The diagrams show Central Library before and after changes were made to its layout.

Clearly, the library has been updated to include dedicated spaces for events and now has an open space in the centre.

Twenty years ago, to the left of the entrance there was a reading room with newspapers and magazines and to the right there was an enquiry desk. Now there's a computer room on the left and a café where the information desk once was. Adult fiction has moved to the right-hand side of the room and all reference books are now on the left. There is a smaller information desk with self-service machines in what once was the adult non-fiction section.

There was a room at the back left-hand corner that had computer games, CDs and videos that has since been enlarged and houses children's fiction. It has a space with two sofas where storytelling events are held. There is a lecture room in the back right-hand corner where children's books used to be.

Here are comments from another examiner:

> This response covers the main changes that have occurred over the 20-year period. An overview is presented in the second paragraph which is quite general: it refers to the [*dedicated spaces for events*] but this could be improved by giving a summary of the key changes (dedicated spaces for events, self-service facilities and a café).

> Ideas are arranged logically: the changes to the front of the library are presented in the third paragraph and the changes to the back section in the final paragraph. This shows a logical approach to reporting the changes and there is some good cohesion [*once was* | *now on the left* | *has since been*].

> There is a good range of vocabulary. In this kind of task, vocabulary from the floor plan needs to be used to report the changes, but the use of different words shows some flexibility and precision [*been updated* | *dedicated spaces* | *houses*].

> In terms of grammar, there are error-free sentences and some variation in structures used when describing changes [*has been updated* | *what once was* | *has since been enlarged*].

> The response could be improved by extending the overview to include more of a summary of the main changes but overall, this response captures the main changes in a logical way.

TEST 3, WRITING TASK 2

This model has been prepared by an examiner as an example of a very good answer.

Statistics show that the world's population is increasing rapidly. It is expected that most of us will be living in cities within the next few decades. The question of whether urbanisation is a positive or negative development remains controversial.

A rapid influx of people moving from rural to urban areas is bound to cause problems. Firstly, pressure on resources such as housing and transportation intensifies. It is becoming difficult for many people to afford adequate housing in cities. A by-product of this is the creation of slums causing low-income families to group together in neglected parts of the city. These people often become trapped in a cycle of poverty that is difficult to escape.

As mentioned above, the growth of urban areas can also lead to severe traffic congestion because more and more vehicles travel into the city from the suburbs. This has many knock-on effects, such as problems with air quality. It also leads many city dwellers to experience mental health issues because travelling across large cities is tiring and stressful.

All of this being said, I don't believe that urbanisation is a wholly negative development. There are advantages to living in large cities that are well managed. For example, there are more schools which means more education opportunities. Access to higher-quality health care is often better in cities. Some cities have also introduced ride-sharing, e-bikes and park and ride services that reduce environmental problems.

My opinion is that many of the problems associated with urbanisation are avoidable but dealing with increasing populations in cities is a formidable challenge. How governments, businesses and society respond to this challenge will dramatically affect the future of our world.

Here are comments from another examiner:

> This response addresses both sides of the question and presents a position, that the movement to cities is not a [*wholly negative development*]. The second and third paragraphs lay out the problems that can be caused by a [*rapid influx*] of people to urban areas [*housing* | *transportation* | *traffic congestion*] and the fourth paragraph presents some of the advantages [*education opportunities* | *higher-quality health care* | *environmental* transport initiatives].

> However, the part of the question about 'the population in the countryside ... decreasing' is not covered. The candidate would need to include it to provide a full answer to this question.

> Information and ideas are logically organised and there is a clear progression, starting with the challenges and ending with a range of advantages.

Vocabulary is used with a natural and sophisticated control [*bound to* | *trapped in a cycle of poverty* | *severe traffic congestion* | *knock-on effects*], although rare errors remain [*education opportunities* / educational opportunities]. Grammar is flexible and accurate, with a wide range of structures included. There are some shorter sentences which could be extended and more multi-clause examples could be included to add complexity.

To improve this response, consideration should be given to the impact of the shrinking population in the countryside.

TEST 4, WRITING TASK 1

This model has been prepared by an examiner as an example of a very good answer.

From the line graph, we can see the average monthly rise or fall in how much copper, nickel and zinc cost throughout 2014.

Overall, nickel started with the highest percentage change of the three but ended with the lowest. Zinc started with the smallest change and ended with the highest, and copper prices fluctuated. Prices for all three metals dipped in June.

In January the price of nickel was up six per cent, but this dropped to negative three percent in June, ending the year with a one percent increase in both November and December. Copper began the year with an increase of two percent and by May, the price was dropping (by slightly less than one per cent). It rose again, increasing by a percentage point in July, August and September. Zinc saw its most dramatic increase in February, with three per cent and the price fell in June (a one percent decrease). The change was negative until October/November when it began to rise.

Here are comments from another examiner:

> This response reports the main data for each of the three metals. There is an introduction in the first paragraph and an overview in the second, followed by the presentation of the main trends of all three categories in the third. Some details are missing (copper after September and no percentage changes for any metal from July to September).

> The candidate identifies the 'dip' for all three in June, but to score more highly, they could also have mentioned that overall, percentage changes fell at the beginning of the year, remained static from July to September and rose after October to the end of the year.

> Information is arranged coherently; each metal is taken in turn for data reporting. There is good use of cohesive devices [*Overall | but | with | when*], but there could be more.

> Vocabulary is adequate with some attempts to use less common items [*fluctuated | dramatic increase*] and attempts to use synonyms [*ended with the lowest | dipped | dropped*].

> There is a lack of complex structures, as most sentences are simple or compound. However, there is some variety in structures, including comparatives [*highest | smallest | most dramatic*] and continuous tenses [*was dropping*].

> To improve the response, the candidate could extend the overview to reflect some common trends and should include some of the missing details.

TEST 4, WRITING TASK 2

This model has been prepared by an examiner as an example of a very good answer.

The population in most parts of the world is ageing; people are living longer and there are fewer younger people in many places as birth rates fall. This phenomenon has pros and cons, but this essay will contend that, on balance, the advantages of having an older population outweigh the negatives.

The first issue that occurs to many people when considering the ageing population is the expense. If people live longer, they may have more than 30 years of retirement and may need to be supported financially by the government or their families. If they experience age-related illness, this impacts the health system and takes up resources needed by other people in society. What's more, when older people are financially independent, it might be hard for younger people if they have to compete to get a foot in the door of the housing market or gain employment.

That being said, older people have a lot to contribute in terms of wisdom, experience and skills. Many people are active and productive for longer than their counterparts were 50 years ago and are an asset to the economy and society well into their old age. They are able to work for longer and after retirement they contribute in many ways too, such as by doing charitable work, spending money as consumers and supporting their families. Grandparents often care for their young grandchildren, making it easier for both parents to work.

While it is true that an ageing population poses challenges for governments, it is clear that these are outweighed by the significant benefits that elderly people bring to society.

Here are comments from another examiner:

> This is a good response to the task. Both sides of the argument are presented, with the ideas extended for both. The candidate makes their position clear from the beginning, that there are more advantages than disadvantages.

> The second paragraph addresses the expense of looking after the elderly, the health system and the cost for governments. It also captures the challenge that older people take up houses and jobs so younger people cannot progress.

> The third paragraph presents the advantages of the [*wisdom, experience and skills*] older people can bring: that they are more active and remain productive for longer, not only working, but also [*doing charitable work, spending money as consumers, supporting their families* and even *grandchildren* for the working parents].

> This means that the conclusion is relevant and justified.

Ideas are organised and cohesion has good progression.

Vocabulary is skilfully used, with some high-level terms [*phenomenon* | *age-related illness* | *impacts the health system*] and some sophisticated examples [*get a foot in the door* | *counterparts*].

There are a range of complex grammatical structures, including several conditional structures [*if*]. The conditionals are used to emphasise the challenges presented and are without errors.

This is a high-level, fully developed response with ideas that are well supported, extended and engaging.

Sample answer sheets

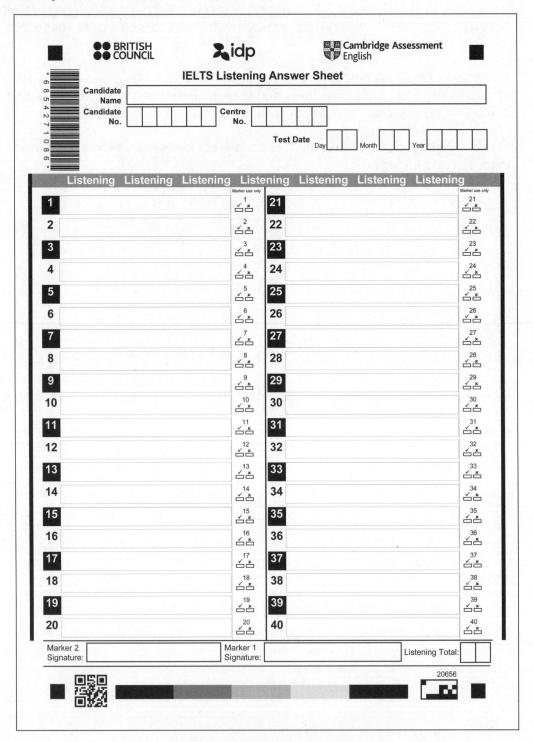

© Cambridge University Press & Assessment 2023

BRITISH COUNCIL **idp** **Cambridge Assessment English**

IELTS Reading Answer Sheet

Candidate Name

Candidate No.

Centre No.

Test Module ☐ Academic ☐ General Training

Test Date Day Month Year

Reading Reading Reading Reading Reading Reading Reading

	Marker use only			Marker use only
1	1 ✓ ✗	21		21 ✓ ✗
2	2 ✓ ✗	22		22 ✓ ✗
3	3 ✓ ✗	23		23 ✓ ✗
4	4 ✓ ✗	24		24 ✓ ✗
5	5 ✓ ✗	25		25 ✓ ✗
6	6 ✓ ✗	26		26 ✓ ✗
7	7 ✓ ✗	27		27 ✓ ✗
8	8 ✓ ✗	28		28 ✓ ✗
9	9 ✓ ✗	29		29 ✓ ✗
10	10 ✓ ✗	30		30 ✓ ✗
11	11 ✓ ✗	31		31 ✓ ✗
12	12 ✓ ✗	32		32 ✓ ✗
13	13 ✓ ✗	33		33 ✓ ✗
14	14 ✓ ✗	34		34 ✓ ✗
15	15 ✓ ✗	35		35 ✓ ✗
16	16 ✓ ✗	36		36 ✓ ✗
17	17 ✓ ✗	37		37 ✓ ✗
18	18 ✓ ✗	38		38 ✓ ✗
19	19 ✓ ✗	39		39 ✓ ✗
20	20	40		40 ✓ ✗

Marker 2 Signature:

Marker 1 Signature:

Reading Total:

61788

BRITISH COUNCIL

idp

Cambridge Assessment English

IELTS Writing Answer Sheet - TASK 1

Candidate Name

Candidate No.

Centre No.

Test Module ☐ Academic ☐ General Training

Test Date Day ☐☐ Month ☐☐ Year ☐☐☐☐

If you need more space to write your answer, use an additional sheet and write in the space provided to indicate how many sheets you are using: Sheet ☐ of ☐

Writing Task 1   Writing Task 1   Writing Task 1   Writing Task 1

Do not write below this line

Do not write in this area. Please continue your answer on the other side of this sheet.

23505

BRITISH COUNCIL **idp** **Cambridge Assessment English**

IELTS Writing Answer Sheet - TASK 2

Candidate Name

Candidate No. Centre No.

Test Module ☐ Academic ☐ General Training   **Test Date** Day Month Year

If you need more space to write your answer, use an additional sheet and write in the space provided to indicate how many sheets you are using: Sheet ☐ of ☐

Writing Task 2 Writing Task 2 Writing Task 2 Writing Task 2

Do not write below this line

Do not write in this area. Please continue your answer on the other side of this sheet.

39507

© Cambridge University Press & Assessment 2023

Acknowledgements

The authors and publishers acknowledge the following sources of copyright material and are grateful for the permissions granted. While every effort has been made, it has not always been possible to identify the sources of all the material used, or to trace all copyright holders. If any omissions are brought to our notice, we will be happy to include the appropriate acknowledgements on reprinting and in the next update to the digital edition, as applicable.

Key: L = Listening; R = Reading.

Text

L1: Sue Watt and *Travel Africa* Magazine for the text adapted from 'How to translocate an elephant' by Sue Watt. Copyright © 2022 *Travel Africa* Magazine. Published by Gecko Publishing Ltd. Reproduced with permission; **R1:** Springer Nature Limited for the text adapted from 'The quest to conquer Earth's space junk problem' by Alexandra Witze, 05.09.2018. Copyright © 2018 Springer Nature Limited. Permission conveyed through Copyright Clearance Center, Inc; *The Guardian* for the text adapted from 'The future of food: Inside the world's largest urban farm – built on a rooftop' by Jon Henley, *The Guardian*, 08.07.2020. Copyright © 2020 Guardian News & Media Limited. Reproduced with permission; The Pennsylvania State University for the text adapted from 'Can cutting your "junk trees" power your city and improve your forest?' by Penn State Extension, 23.04.2015. Copyright © 2015 The Pennsylvania State University. Reproduced with kind permission; **R2:** A&E Networks for the text adapted from 'British history – Stonehenge', 03.02.2020. Copyright © 2020 A&E Television Networks LLC. All rights reserved. Reproduced with permission; Alessandro Melis for the text adapted from 'Leonardo da Vinci designed an ideal city that was centuries ahead of its time' by Alessandro Melis, *The Conversation*, 03.05.2019. Copyright © 2019 Alessandro Melis. Reproduced with kind permission; Huw Price and Karina Vold for the text adapted from 'Research horizons – artificial intelligence' by Huw Price and Karina Vold. Copyright © University of Cambridge, www.cam.ac.uk. Reproduced with kind permission; **R3:** Alan Bellows for the text adapted from 'The last great steam car' by Alan Bellows. Copyright © 2006 Damn Interesting. Reproduced with permission; Aeon Media Group Ltd for the text adapted from 'Why streaming kids according to ability is a terrible idea' by Oscar Hedstrom, 03.05.2019. Copyright © 2019 Aeon Media Group Ltd. Reproduced with kind permission; *The Guardian* for the text adapted from 'Ply in the sky: the new materials to take us beyond concrete' by Fiona Harvey, *The Guardian*, 27.02.2019. Copyright © 2019 Guardian News & Media Limited. Reproduced with permission; **R4:** Aeon Media Group Ltd for the text adapted from 'The growth mindset problem' by Carl Hendrick, 11.03.2019. Copyright © 2019 Aeon Media Group Ltd. Reproduced with permission; Michael Hardman and Nick Davies for the text adapted from 'Green roofs improve the urban environment – so why don't all buildings have them?' by Michael Hardman and Nick Davies, *The Conversation*, 04.10.2019. Copyright © 2019 Michael Hardman and Nick Davies. Reproduced with kind permission.

Audio

Audio production by dsound recording Ltd.

Typesetting

Typesetting by QBS Learning.

URLs

The publisher has used its best endeavours to ensure that the URLs for external websites referred to in this book are correct and active at the time of going to press. However, the publisher has no responsibility for the websites and can make no guarantee that a site will remain live or that the content is or will remain appropriate.

Practice Makes Perfect

By teachers for teachers

Get more out of Authentic Practice Tests

Lesson Plans

Teacher Tips

Extra Support

- Get Tips and Tricks to use in your classroom
- Download practice test Lesson Plans
- Explore the extra support, training and technology available for your exam

Find out more at
practicemakesperfect.cambridge.org